W9-DFR-989

POSITIVE
DISCIPLINE

POSITIVE

DISCIPLINE

James Menzies Black

American Management Association, Inc.

CARNEGIE LIBRARY
LIVINGSTONE COLLEGE
SALISBURY, N. C

© American Management Association, Inc., 1970
All rights reserved. Printed in the United States of America.

This book may not be reproduced in whole or in part
without the express permission of the Association.

International standard book number: 0-8144-5227-2
Library of Congress catalog card number: 70-121834

FIRST PRINTING

658.3129
B627

87599

CONTENTS

CONTENTS

POSITIVE
DISCIPLINE

1

DECADE OF DILEMMA

Discipline in a Changing Society

MEN YEARN FOR DISCIPLINE most when there is an absence of it. Yet, when American historians of some future day write of contemporary society, they will note that it was a period of revolutionary change, of swiftly advancing technology, of hitherto undreamed affluence, and of a widespread breakdown in traditional values and social discipline.

In an era pockmarked by violence, riots, and organized flouting of civil law, the values of reasoned and cooperative discipline are sometimes lost sight of in the laissez-faire code of social permissiveness. And therein lies the greatest danger to our economic system and our civilization. Human beings cannot exist or work together unless they accept rules of discipline of their own making or have such rules imposed upon them by the power of absolute government. The acceptance by people of reasonable and positive disciplinary regulations encourages individualism and personal and group achievement. But, inevitably, if human beings refuse to take the responsibility for disciplining their own lives and playing their part in maintaining an orderly society, discipline will be impressed upon them by dictatorial authority. The sad part of it is that so often the authority of totalitarian leadership, at least initially, has been willingly granted by a majority who have abdicated their accountability for self-rule but are angrily tired of disorder.

The Other Side of the Coin

The obverse side of the coin of anarchy is tyranny, and the very word "tyranny" implies negative and punitive disciplinary measures. Even a casual reading of history will demonstrate the frequency with which men, no longer able to conduct their own affairs, have vested total powers in dictatorships which promise to restore normality and order. Absolute governments of the right or the left have arisen to cure the anarchic sicknesses of nations; but the methods they have used, regardless of their motivating philosophies, have been essentially the same. They have employed without exception the tool of ruthless suppression, and people under their control have obeyed their disciplinary laws or received instant and severe punishment.

Although it is easy to grant absolute power, once it is bestowed it is seldom lightly relinquished. Dictatorships, once established, are seldom overthrown from within except by other dictatorships. And people who give up their tradition of liberty are likely to become accustomed to autocratic rule. Eventually, they may prefer it to freedom since it relieves them of the problems of self-discipline.

A quick examination of the past will reveal the alarming tendency of humanity to abandon personal liberty for strong, government-imposed order. Julius Caesar found conditions in the Roman Republic, tortured as it was by violence and civil war, made to order for a take-over which he eventually accomplished. Caesar was successful in restoring order, but he laid the foundation for a succession of absolute emperors whose rule lasted until Rome itself was overthrown by warlike barbarians.

Napoleon was welcomed by the French, who were tired and frightened by the excesses of the Revolution, because they hoped his rule would bring an end to domestic turmoil. This Napoleon accomplished, but the price was heavy. Frenchmen died by the thousands on battlefields from Spain to Russia, and there are experts who say that the heavy drain on her manpower started France on her decline as a major power. True, Napoleon was at last defeated and died in exile. But again it was not the people of France who toppled him in search of their lost liberties. It was the armies of other nations allied against a feared dictator.

Adolf Hitler discovered the environment of the Weimar Republic ideal for his movement of national socialism. The permissiveness of the government, plus the failure of the public to react when Hitler's gangs of hoodlum brownshirts broke up meetings of opposition groups, terrorized universities, and physically maltreated professors whose points of view were counter to their own, assured the success of the Nazis. Once in power, Hitler clamped an iron rule on his people; and discipline, symbolized by the goose-step cadence of marching men, effectively stilled any opposition.

While the Russian Revolution was not an example of the overthrow of a democratic government in any sense of the word, it is still a fact of history that the Russian people were relieved when the bloody battles between the Red armies and the armies of the counterrevolutionaries ended. After years of chaos men and women wanted peace; and the price of peace and order was not too high, at least at first, even if it meant the dictatorship of Stalin.

The Climate of Backlash

Against this background it is perhaps easier to understand the problems in every area of our society that must be solved—and, if we are to continue in the tradition of liberty and self-discipline, solved in a manner that assures the freedom of institutions, organizations, and individuals. If we fail to impose discipline on ourselves, eventually it will be done for us. The love of order and normality is instinctive. While to some the excitement that may be found in taking part in group defiance of constituted authority may be stimulating, while such defiance may inflate the egos of young people who take over college administration buildings from bewildered and permissive college deans and presidents, while it may give other people a sense of power to rampage through the streets and put the torch to cities, all these people are merely playing at revolution. They have committed their undisciplined acts without fear of reprisal; indeed, sometimes they have apparently been protected by the very forces of law and order that in other days would have reacted in a drastically different manner.

Sociologists and psychologists have written lengthily, excusing and explaining the behavior of violence. And, while such explanations may have merit, increasingly they are receiving less attention from a public which is suffering from the excesses of the undisciplined and paying heavy taxes to support what, in some cases, might almost be termed government-subsidized acts of violence. If the official climate of permissiveness permits the continuation of anarchy, the vast majority of the public will respond by giving support to leaders who promise to take stern measures to restore tranquillity. To accomplish their goals, leaders of this kind may resort to harsh and unpleasant methods to which historically we are unaccustomed. We may lose our individual rights permanently by attempting to cure what could be temporary wrongs arbitrarily. But, under the pressure of emergency, the majority of men and women are not noted for their ability to think objectively. All too often their plea is "Do something now. Do anything you please. But get the job done. We'll worry about what happens next tomorrow."

The Influence of Government

The government during these affluent years has itself appeared at times to pursue a policy of permissiveness calculated to bring about an almost chaotic condition in practically every metropolitan area in the nation. Badly needed legislation to correct social wrongs has been enacted, but too often the implementation of these laws has been in the hands of theorists and ideologists, some of whom, seemingly, are professed enemies of free enterprise and private initiative and who sometimes appear to seek to destroy liberty in the name of progress. Unfortunately they have tended to promise more than they could deliver, with the result that people to whom the promises have been made have lost faith in what they describe as "the establishment," and the violence of their reaction has been evident in riots, demonstrations, and civil disobedience. It is ironic that statutes designed to bring about a more cohesive and equitable society appear to have resulted in what amounts to its fractionalization into bitterly contesting groups which so distrust each other that it is difficult to reestablish workable channels of communication among them.

The Social Responsibility of Industry

In a modern technological society, wealth depends on the productivity and creativity of industry, which in turn must have the normality of order that is based on positive and cooperative discipline to remain competitive or even to exist. Management has evolved effective methods to achieve organizational harmony. Using the expert knowledge of behavioral scientists, it has designed programs assuring sensible employee selection, sound placement, continuous training, educational advantages, and promotional opportunities for the ambitious and the competent. Supervisors and executives, aside from the training they receive in their specialized fields, have been thoroughly schooled in leadership methods. Alert companies have developed a wide variety of programs designed to improve the communication abilities, the teaching skills, and the economic understanding of their leadership. Participative management has been emphasized, and the ideas, suggestions, and recommendations of employees at all organizational levels are not only listened to but encouraged.

Leading American companies are jealous of their public reputation and pride themselves on their social consciousness. They support educational institutes and community projects with money, time, and the talents of their executives. At almost any meeting of businessmen and industry leaders you hear phrases like "the social conscience of industry" and "management's civic responsibility" intermingled in discussions of such managerial problems as sales, production, and finances. Supervisors and executives are constantly reminded of their public relations obligations and urged to take part in outside activities that enhance the public image of their companies.

In accomplishing its objectives, industry has been startlingly successful. It has poured an abundance of wealth into the American economy and created a society which, despite an increasingly heavy tax load, inflation, and profligate spending by both the public and the government, is affluent beyond the most imaginative predictions of turn-of-the-century economists. Of course, there have been temporary setbacks, periods when business has faltered for a while in its forward momentum or has even retreated. But, by and large, the economy has moved steadily ahead in achieving greater and greater prosperity for the majority of Americans.

In the process, however, the very forces that made this progress possible have been weakened by the wealth they have produced—at least the effect of that wealth on people, especially younger persons who accept affluence as the normal state of things. While they are pleased to use money to further their own interests, idealistic or otherwise, too many of them would appear to look with contempt or indifference on the machinery that provides it. The Horatio Alger myth, which reflected the social attitudes of an industrial society in its infancy, has disappeared along with the Puritan ethic that adjured people to work and produce. Parents have been able to provide their children with educational advantages that were once reserved for the wealthy few, but these same parents have too often neglected their responsibility for inculcating in those children a sense of personal responsibility. Institutions that were formerly regarded as sources of moral and spiritual values and sanctuaries of enlightened and reasoned discussion are themselves in a state of change that is almost upheaval and have provided no consistent or decisive leadership.

The Symptoms of Breakdown

Any management textbook provides a list of what are classed as signs of the breakdown of discipline within an organization. This list includes absenteeism, low productivity, a rise in grievances, unrest, insubordination, slowdowns, work stoppages, and mass picketing. If these are indeed symptoms of the disintegration of discipline, it takes no expert to diagnose the malady from which this nation suffers.

A leadership that seeks to purchase gratitude from special groups which receive its bounties and subsidies, that attempts to appease and placate instead of administering fair and consistent justice, that bases decisions on expediency and wishful thinking rather than on hard reality, will lose the respect of all and even earn the contempt of those it has favored most. It can hold its power only so long as it has the money to pay ransom for its authority, and every passing year that power will diminish.

When pressure groups learn that they have only to use the threat of force to get what they seek, their demands become more and more extreme until at last they are defined as "basic and nonnegotiable." When civil discipline has declined to such a state that mob violence suffers no reprisal —in fact, is actually able to achieve its goals—conditions have been allowed to degenerate to such a state that what amounts to an unguided and nihilistic revolution is in being. Moreover, the goals of such a revolution are nebulous or so inadequately defined that they are understood neither by its leaders nor by their followers. But, in a society where a church once thought to be an anchor is no longer certain where it stands, where to many people such once-respected symbols of law and order as the fireman and the policeman are objects of contempt and hatred, where courts concerned with social justice tend to ignore their traditional role of firmly and objectively administering the law, the environment is not conducive to disciplined and orderly processes of group action.

Curiously enough, the affluence that we Americans have achieved underwrites the very conditions about which we complain. The man who is financially secure himself hesitates to take a personal risk and dreads to do anything that might diminish his prosperity. It is easier to pay somebody else to take the responsibility—and, in the safe seclusion of the home, to deplore the situation with "think the same way" friends who also play the part of concerned but do-nothing spectators.

The late humorist Will Rogers remarked during the

depression of the early thirties that Americans were the only people who could afford to drive to the poorhouse in their automobiles. If he were alive today, he might observe that Americans are the only people who support with money fellow citizens, young and old, whose manners they find objectionable, whose methods they abhor, whose dress they think is repulsive, and whose stated object in some instances is to destroy them along with the "false values" of their "materialistic, bourgeois social system."

The Middle Class and Traditional Values

We have allowed some of these conditions to develop by shrugging off the duties to both family and community that our less sophisticated parents and grandparents assumed as normal obligations. In rejecting personal involvement, we rationalize that we have acquired the gift of tolerance, whereas apathy or indifference might be more descriptive of our attitude. In the pursuit of "togetherness," families actually create the generation gap because they take no note of the maxim that familiarity breeds contempt and that no man is a hero to his valet. In striving to understand and be understood by our children, we abandon our right to respect and authority in a futile attempt to become playmates of our kiddies and cocktail-party companions of our teenagers.

Students from well-to-do homes enter college sure of receiving ample allowances from home and expect as a matter of course to be provided with automobiles and vacation trips to Europe—or at least to make the scene at the beaches of Fort Lauderdale or wherever the action is. When they graduate, they are reasonably certain, well-paying jobs will be available when they get around to working at them. And, because they are accustomed to instant gratification of their desires, some of them lack the persistence and self-control to accept even temporary reverses. Social scientists report that a large percentage of students who become hippies or leaders of radical student activist movements are the product of middle-class homes who are still financed by parents whose values and standards they have rejected but whose money they welcome.

Of course, these observations are generalizations. The great majority of Americans, both young and old, continue to live by long-accepted standards of conduct and continue to raise their families in the normal manner, to work at their jobs, to respect authority and traditional moral standards. But, unfortunately, this majority—and it is an exceedingly large one—no longer appears to play the deciding role in creating the national climate of morality. The average American receives very little attention. It is the activities of the undisciplined that get the headlines and supply material for the comments of telecasters.

This is not unusual. Will Durant once observed that when Rome was in its degenerate decline the average middle-class Roman was still living with his wife, providing a decent home for his children, and conducting his affairs in the usual way. But his influence on the conduct of the state and on standards of morality and discipline decreased with each succeeding year.

The Problems to Be Solved

In spite of this country's affluence, it still has many social problems—including poverty and lack of opportunity for large groups of Americans, particularly minority groups. Although great effort and much money have been devoted to the solution of these difficulties, any real solution appears more distant now than ever before, probably because for the first time we are seeing the total extent of the dilemma. However, behavioral scientists practically all agree that failure to understand or accept middle-class standards of discipline is a major factor in the inability of the underprivileged to take advantage of the training and education offered and so become a part of the nation's productive mainstream.

Commenting on this question, Sir W. Arthur Lewis, himself a Negro, wrote in Princeton's *University* magazine ("Black Power and the American University," Spring 1969), "The problem of the black will remain essentially the same—that problem being whether he is going to be mostly in the bottom jobs or whether he will get his 11 percent share of the top and middle. And his chance at the top is going to depend on his getting into those select schools and getting the same kind of technical education that whites are getting."

Sir Arthur went on to say, "Those black leaders who wish us to concentrate our efforts on working for revolution in America are living on a myth, for our problems and needed strategies are going to be exactly the same whether there is a revolution or not. In the integrated part of the American economy our essential strategy has been to use all the normal channels of advancement—the high schools, apprenticeships, night schools; it is only by climbing this ladder that the black man is going to escape from his concentration in the bottom job of the economy."

Such hard-minded advice receives too few listeners because it does not permit easy solutions and provides no crash training programs that turn ghetto youths into productive and highly paid employees almost overnight. It is much simpler for the demagogue to retreat from reality and offer utopia on terms that appeal to the basest instincts of his constituency. But in an era of abundance people are not psychologically receptive to "blood, sweat, and tears" exhortations. And so what actually amounts almost to the polarization of society along racial lines continues; and in such an environment positive and cooperative discipline, without which competitive industry cannot long succeed, is extremely hard to attain.

Sir Arthur takes note of the need for discipline and offers this advice to his own people. "The secret is to inspire our young people with confidence in their potential achievement. And psychologists tell us that the background to this is a warm and secure family life. The most successful minorities in America, the Chinese, the Japanese, and the Jews, are distinguished by their close and highly disciplined family—which is the exact opposite of what has now become the stereotype. . . . Given a disciplined family life and open doors to opportunity, I have no doubt that American blacks will capture one field after another, as fast as barriers come down."

The Example of Leadership

Sir Arthur's thinking makes solid sense, and it can be studied profitably by white as well as black Americans. National pride and democratic progress depend on the self-imposed discipline of people, and the discipline of the individual is inspired by the example that is set by his leaders—in his home, at his school, in government, and at his place of work.

This last poses a great problem for industry. More and more the public and government are turning to management for help in reducing the tremendous burden of the taxpayer by employing persons who are dependent on welfare. This challenge industry is meeting, but the introduction into the workforce of men and women who must be supervised by different sets of standards, at least initially, immediately causes disciplinary problems and, sometimes, friction between regular employees who believe in traditional values and the new ones who may not even understand them, much less accept them.

Modern management has long understood that positive discipline is achieved through positive leadership, and its executive and supervisory educational programs have striven to provide its managers with the training they require to direct people. But formerly there were essentially no class bars between the leaders and the led. Both talked the same language, accepted the same standards, possessed the same values. The leader, therefore, could identify objectives to his group and depend on their pride, ambition, and self-interest to help him accomplish them.

The employee himself was highly motivated. No government agency dragged him from a ghetto street, sent him to training school, and then helped him to find a job which he was given, not because he was qualified, but because he was disadvantaged. No company sent a representative looking for him to persuade him to accept employment. He suffered no glaring educational deficiencies; and, while his ambitions might not soar to such heights as becoming the company's president or even a manager, he did look forward to advancement and to the same type of suburban living that his superiors enjoyed. Finally, he knew there was no arbitrary or discriminatory line drawn against his upward progress and that the opportunity for promotion was open to him.

People who are self-motivated and interested in their work respond readily to intelligent discipline. It is those who have for too long been rootless, undirected, and idle who reject controls even of their own making. Therefore, to attempt to absorb large numbers of such persons into what have hitherto been highly disciplined organizations is bound to create social, economic, and leadership problems of startling dimensions.

Industry is not government. Its philosophy is pragmatic, not political. Its solutions to problems are realistic, not impractically idealistic. Therefore, it would be a disservice to the public and to the disadvantaged to build up false hopes about what companies can do in curing social ills that have been building up for generations.

The Challenge to Industry

This does not mean that management cannot play a responsible and constructive role in overcoming some of the difficulties that this country faces. Jenkin Lloyd Jones, when he became president of the U.S. Chamber of Commerce, soberly reflected on the actions industry could take.

"One thing the business community of America can do is to increase opportunity to escape the poverty cycle. It can if it gets cooperation from the unions and ends discriminatory practices. It can increase on-the-job training for better jobs. It can support educational programs, not merely for technical training, but for giving the so-called hard core the basic skills for simple and repetitive jobs. But business cannot supply motivation. When the door is open, the individual himself must walk through. He cannot expect to be carried. This may have been understressed in the past. Too many people, perhaps, have been told that the way to a better life lies by demand, riot, and mindless commotion. If these people continue to be misled—and if the majority of Americans react with backlash and disgust —then we'll all be worse off."

Mr. Jones is referring to a comparatively small group when he speaks of the "hard core" in describing the problem that must be solved before such people can be integrated into the mainstream of productive American life. Moreover, "backlash from the right" is generally due to lack of leadership from the middle, and that is now beginning to assert itself. Fortunately, the great majority of the American people who make up the so-called center are moderate and self-disciplined. They still respond to constructive, rational leadership and have it within their power to assert values that will have an ameliorating effect on the permissive climate of the country in which so many traditional values are being challenged and, often, needlessly destroyed. While constructive change is ever necessary, for true progress there should always be intelligent guidance; nihilistic solutions to even manifest wrongs are an open invitation to tyranny.

Industry, facing the most dynamic social challenge that it has encountered, will need the understanding and support of all moderate Americans if it is to render a useful service in overcoming the nation's social ills. To gain such understanding and support calls for the opening up of more and more channels of communication between management and the public. For example, the public will have to understand precisely what problems a company faces when it attempts to train disadvantaged people and exactly what results can reasonably be attained. There must be no wishful thinking on the part of anybody; and the greater the degree to which middle-class America itself becomes involved in the question, the better will be the chance for an eventual solution.

Perhaps one cause of our present difficulties is the past attitude of the public, including its willingness to leave everything to the government, whose solution to any problem is generally to develop programs and spend money. It is clearly evident that this has not worked; and, although billions of dollars are being spent and programs have expanded and proliferated, the problems have constantly increased in size and complexity.

When General Joseph Stillwell and his army got a severe trouncing from the Japanese during World War II and had to retreat from Burma to the safety of India, he did not hide behind excuses. He said, "I say we got the hell kicked out of us. Now we must find out what we did wrong, plan how to do better, and go back in and win."

This might not be a bad time for the people of this country to make their own reappraisal. They can no more expect industry to do the job of curing social ills solely by its own efforts than they could expect government to cure them. In the long run, the only people who can supply the drive and the desire to improve the lot of the poor are the poor themselves, but at present they often lack both of these qualities. Such attributes can be instilled, but it will take leadership of the highest quality to do so. And

17

that leadership must come from all groups in society working together to achieve definite and reachable objectives. Easy concepts that find words in such promises as "40 acres and a mule," "every man a king," and "instant prosperity through superficial training" may win the support of the poor, but when they prove impossible of fullfillment this support is bound to turn to anger and frustration.

In this kind of mood the difficulty of doing anything for the disadvantaged will be harder than ever. Will Durant, in his histories of various civilizations and nations, remarks on the frequency with which men try to vote themselves to riches, but he adds that the attempt inevitably causes greater bitterness, greater confusion, and greater strife. The Puritan ethic may not be as appealing as it has been in days past, but it is still a straight road to self-discipline, individualism, and the self-initiative of democracy. If a nation loses its sense of personal responsibility and has discipline imposed on it, each citizen will lose a right that is infinitely more precious—the privilege of free initiative. And industry will lose the creativity of participative management which has enabled it to produce so much for so many and, instead, become a creature of all-powerful government.

Modern industry has a tremendous social responsibility, but it still must function in a competitive environment; it still must depend on organizational efficiency and the force of positive discipline to accomplish its objectives. Enlightened industrial relations practices assure justice to employees and protect them from arbitrary, punitive, or capricious management decisions that would be harmful to their interests. The right to dissent is guaranteed by official procedures; in fact, the concept of union-management relations is based on the theory that the two parties have more in common than in conflict. Intelligent companies welcome differences in points of view and the free discussion of ideas. But, after the varying opinions on proposals have been carefully considered, and when final decisions have been made, everyone connected with the organization must work together cooperatively to implement them effectively. Any other course would be suicidally against the interests of the group as a whole.

Industry must seek realistic solutions to problems, even social problems. It cannot afford to promise results that are impossible to achieve. People who are brought into an organization must be taught how to become productive members of it and how to accept the discipline of the group. Obviously it will take leadership of the highest caliber to gain these ends.

The Alienated

The young idealist who lives in the security of his family's economic protection relies on his emotions to solve long-standing ills which he sees in the nation's economic and social system. Rhetoric and vengeful action are always easier than developing rational alternatives. But people who incline toward the easy way are scarcely prepared for the discipline of industry. Neither by training nor inclination have they the desire to direct their idealism, if such it is, into constructive channels where eventually, by hard work and ability, they could conceivably arrive in positions where they would have the power and knowledge to apply remedies to problems that now they can only dimly and incoherently identify. When they find themselves—as

19

they sometimes do—in secure niches in government, teaching, or even business, they may attempt to apply their theories; but unfortunately they seldom possess the stamina in the face of challenge or the self-discipline to reject idealistic solutions to basic problems, even when it can be demonstrated that such solutions will not win public support and cannot be enforced by fiat.

The disadvantaged, of course, are in no respect similar to their idealistic allies, nor are their difficulties the same. The lack of self-discipline in the former is due to poverty, ignorance, and inability to understand or accept values and standards that persons brought up in a middle-class tradition take for granted. The hard-core unemployed, who may have subsisted on various government welfare programs for three generations, cannot be expected to take readily to training that would impose regular hours on them and force them to undergo orderly instruction that would provide them with the basic skills which industry requires. Lacking education, frequently even the ability to read and write, they have difficulty seeing the advantage of being prepared to do a job that at best could be considered semiskilled when the wages they earn for such work are not much more than they already get from the government. Further, their very environment makes them receptive to the oratory of demagogues who promise immediate social benefits and who stimulate and manipulate their followers by the excitement of participation in violent action that can accomplish nothing except mindless destruction.

On the one hand, therefore, we have an educated segment of society—including many younger people—which has rejected its traditional values and on the other the disadvantaged, the ghetto dwellers and the rural poor, the chronically unemployed who have never possessed such values in the first place. Both groups are alienated from what most people consider the mainstream of society, and both are hard if not impossible to communicate with: the anti-establishment college graduate because of opposition based on ideological and doctrinaire grounds and the disadvantaged because (particularly if he is a Negro) he has been discriminated against in the past and at present probably lacks the education and technical skills that would make him competitive in what he may contemptuously refer to as the "honky power structure."

Unfortunately, both groups have been so little restrained by government, and have so often been encouraged by the press and by liberal faculty members of prestige universities, that they tend to seek solutions to every problem by the exercise of force. The resulting breakdown of ordinary discipline in many areas of American society is a hallmark of the past decade. The very phrase "law and order" in some quarters is considered a cryptic anti-Negro slogan, and the so-called "soul" courses distinguished universities have instituted to appease black militants have neither appeased them nor equipped them to live and prosper in a modern technological society.

Bayard Rustin, the distinguished Negro educator, made this point when he pleaded with university officials "to stop capitulating to the . . . Negroes and see that they get the remedial training that they need." Rustin concluded, "What in the hell are soul courses worth in the real world? In the real world, who gives a damn if you have taken soul courses? They want to know if you can do mathematics and write a correct sentence."

Selling the Opportunity for Accomplishment

Industry, unlike the opportunistic politician or demagogue, cannot take the cheap way out by pledging easy answers to complex questions. It must, through its leadership, ally itself with the great majority of the American public and work along practical lines to accomplish realistic goals. If it is true that the young idealist in college is antibusiness—a statement which is often heard but may be debatable—leaders of business should do a better job of selling the industry story, not of success but of accomplishment, on the college campus. Where but in industry can a young man who finally reaches a top executive position continue even in his late middle age to build, to create more job opportunities, to provide the money and the technical knowledge that will eliminate slums and turn the unemployed into producers?

A challenge of this kind should certainly appeal to the college graduate who can couple his idealism with constructive self-discipline and who understands that knowledge of a field plus the ability to apply theory to practical situations is necessary to achievement in any endeavor. After all, Henry Ford, regardless of his motivation, created more permanent job opportunities for more people and, in so doing, gave them a higher standard of living than government "make work" programs which may be necessary for short-term purposes but accomplish little of lasting value—much less instilling the pride of attainment in the workers who have participated in them.

It may be worth commenting on the fact that campus unrest has seldom won the active support of students pursuing hard, rigorous disciplines, such as medicine, engineering, or the pure sciences, which demand time and energy to master successfully and which prepare one for a profession. The college rebel has come mostly from the ranks of liberal arts majors, especially those in social studies, many of whom appear to lack direction and concrete goals and so occupy themselves with brainstorming solutions to social evils and come up with answers which are as impractical as their originators are inexperienced. The intellectual potential of many of these people is beyond dispute. But, sadly, they risk failure to realize their possibilities simply because they refuse to equip themselves for the very careers which most appeal to them.

Pablo Picasso, a master of abstract painting, won a reputation as an artist by painting in a traditional manner and was thoroughly adept in line, form, and color before he began to experiment. Just so, the successful radical is a highly disciplined person; and, though he may use undisciplined adherents to his cause as shock troops, he eliminates them as a threat to the new order he establishes as soon as his purpose has been achieved. Some young people today openly proclaim that they are reactionaries starting out on their journey to revolution before they have packed their intellectual suitcases with the intellectual equipment that would make them useful to a revolution.

Industry, today, is faced with a severe test that is both economic and social. It must maintain an efficient, competitive, creative organization that relies on the self-discipline of its individual members to attain results. And it must continue to attract young people who have the ability, intelligence, and desire to become the leaders of industry tomorrow. Finally, in addition to the employment of what are essentially middle-class people for its staff positions and regular jobs, it must absorb large numbers of persons who have hitherto lived totally apart from society's mainstream and who have values and standards that are different from those of America's vast majority and who lack the education, skills, and self-discipline—and sometimes even the will—to achieve success in a competitive industrial environment.

As if these deficiencies in themselves were not enough to overcome, disadvantaged minority citizens suffer from the irresponsibility of many of their leaders. These men preach hostility to the establishment and promise shortcuts to riches through the use of force—by which, they say, they can exact recompense for past wrongs, perhaps even enabling their followers to establish a state within a state. Such proposals are impossible of attainment, but this does not lessen their appeal to people who have been stirred up emotionally and cannot be expected to welcome "nuts and bolts" programs based on hard work when their objectives can seemingly be won by other and more exciting methods.

To take a person from such an environment and instill in him the attitudes and motivation that are necessary for accomplishment in organized industry is a monumental undertaking, especially when, like as not, such a person returns each day to a ghetto home where his associates have views and modes of living that are completely opposite from those of his fellow employees at the company. This is not to say that he cannot be trained to perform useful jobs or that it is impossible to teach him the worth of those standards that the middle class takes for granted. It does mean that industry cannot do the job alone, nor can it easily introduce large numbers of undisciplined, untrained people into an organization all at once without destroying the morale and efficiency of the organization itself.

To attract the leadership it requires for the future, industry will have to revamp and redirect its recruitment activities. It must place more emphasis on the constructive achievements of business in terms of the social and material benefits it renders to society as a whole. This is not to say that the competitive nature of management should be played down or that the company function of returning a profit should be ignored. But to take part in fair competition should be an invitation to the ambitious, and an examination of the record will reveal the many constructive uses to which company profits have been turned.

So far as absorbing the disadvantaged is concerned, this will not be done overnight or by any series of crash programs. The training must be careful and thorough and must be conducted by persons qualified by knowledge and by motivation to give it. Moreover, industry cannot accomplish this training task by itself. So long as the leadership of government is permissive, the public is apathetic, and society's laws are not respected, training many of the undisciplined, poorly motivated disadvantaged will be almost impossible. An unnamed Negro educator was quoted by a metropolitan newspaper as remarking in the aftermath of a riot, "It is hard to persuade black youth to work to get a color television when they can break into stores and take them untroubled by the police who stand by as spectators."

Industry is certainly conscious of its social responsibility. Already many leading companies have developed programs designed to bring hard-core people into useful employment. Already these companies have learned much from experience.

The vice-president of a Pittsburgh manufacturer whose company has achieved remarkable results in this direction comments, "An employer who sets out to build a training program for ghetto people should know exactly what he is doing. The selection of who is to be trained should be meticulous and careful, not in terms of traditional factors such as education, experience, and proven ability, but from the point of view of motivation. Here the behaviorial sciences are useful. Tests can help you detect motivation. If the people who are brought into the initial program have the will to achieve or that will can be built into them and they receive instruction from patient, skillful instructors who have themselves received training regarding the attitudes and problems of the students, a good percentage of the trainees will be successful. They will eventually become your best recruiters, and their example will be more persuasive than all the arguments and preachments of leaders of government and industry."

The Meaning of Positive Discipline

Yes, the problem of how to operate an efficient, productive organization will become more complex as technology produces more and more well-paid leisure for more and more people. If predictions about the America of tomorrow are accurate (some prophets claim that by the year 2000 the workweek will be reduced to four hours and poverty will be largely eliminated), material rewards or even fringe benefits will not in themselves provide the incentive that will prod the ambitious to accomplishment and the average to satisfactory performance. Money and security will be almost taken for granted. Motivations of another kind will be required.

But predictions of utopian tomorrows have a habit of straying off course, and 2000 A.D. is still over the horizon.

In the meantime management must rely on the skill of its own leadership to maintain organizational effectiveness.

Perhaps, then, if industry is to continue to attract highly motivated people who will work together in an organization, it must offer the incentive of becoming a self-respecting, productive citizen to the hard-core minority citizen and the young college graduate alike through the opportunity to move forward in a career that will offer the chance of personal accomplishment and public service. Group self-discipline is gained when the members of the group and its leadership have mutual goals. And individual self-discipline is the foundation of democratic government and, for that matter, participative management.

It is unfortunate that the very word "discipline" is often thought of in its narrow and punitive sense. When discipline is synonymous with punishment, it is entirely negative. Discipline should be a constructive, positive force that enables people to work together harmoniously. Consider the word affirmatively and its full meaning becomes evident. Discipline to the scholar is a field of study which, if mastered, hardens or toughens his mind. The football coach refers to a championship team as "well disciplined," meaning that it executes its plays with precision and skill. A highly trained regiment of soldiers is proud of its reputation for being disciplined; to the soldiers, discipline means that everybody knows his job and each individual works cooperatively with the group to carry out orders. In such an organization the members themselves enforce the rules of discipline, and penalties for breaching them seldom need to be imposed.

The task of management, therefore, is to create the climate in which employees are encouraged to accept the leadership of executives and supervisors and to show their acceptance by efficient performance. If this is accomplished, morale and productivity are high. People *like* discipline; they like to be part of a successful group and are proud of the reputation they earn thereby. The fact that a person can meet the standards of an organization known for its high standards is a source of satisfaction to him. A good employee transferred to a unit where discipline is lax will soon lose his drive and effectiveness. His morale will drop, and by his very attitude he will show that what he really misses is the discipline of the successful unit of which he was once a member.

The problem of discipline is complex and comprised of all the lights and shadows of human nature itself. And the question of how to convert a group of individuals, each with different motivations, ambitions, skills, and aptitudes, into a disciplined, cooperative working group is a constant challenge to management. Times change and conditions change, but human nature remains essentially the same. Therefore, the development of positive discipline brings into play every management skill; for discipline, defined thus, is really management itself.

The experienced executive or supervisor is well aware of the many opportunities he has to develop self-discipline in his people. The manager is introducing an employee to positive discipline when he trains him to do his job efficiently and explains how it is to his advantage to work cooperatively with his fellows to accomplish common goals.

It is part of discipline to encourage employees to develop their talents and skills and to acquire attitudes and build patterns of behavior that earn self-respect. It also is part of discipline to teach employees how to discipline their thinking and working methods so that they will become more self-reliant and have greater initiative.

Finally, it is an obligation of a manager to use his authority to bring persons who transgress discipline back into harmony with the group. This he does by counsel and persuasion, by warning, or, as a last resort, by punishment. Even in this sense, the objective of the manager is—not to punish for the sake of punishment—but to force the erring group members to realize the necessity of working within the boundaries of sensible rules and regulations.

Here are six suggestions for building positive self-discipline in employee attitudes.

1. *Think like a manager.* To be a leader, it is necessary to think like a leader and have the attitudes of leadership. A manager must earn the respect and confidence of subordinates because of his ability, judgment, and impartiality. The executive or supervisor who bases his management of people on these qualities will help the members of his group develop self-discipline.

2. *Set high standards.* It has been said that the job of a manager is to train average people to do superior jobs. This means he must set high standards and train employees in how to meet them. Encouragement, recognition, and coaching are the tools he uses to develop the productive capability of his group.

3. *Train carefully.* Self-discipline is built into the working habits of a well-trained employee unit. For discipline means knowledge. Not only is the untrained or half-trained employee unproductive, but his attitude may be hostile. He resents his own shortcomings and resents a manager who will tolerate poor performance. In all likelihood, such an employee will vent his hostility on the superior who refuses to give him the training he requires for satisfactory performance.

4. *Communicate intelligently.* Begin on the day a new

employee starts work to introduce him to the discipline of the group. Explain the how and why of company rules and regulations. Give the newcomer the instruction, counsel, and encouragement he needs to meet job standards even if this means providing him with special coaching or personal attention. So far as the group as a whole is concerned, keep it advised on company policy and problems, especially reasons for changes in policies. Encourage suggestions, and make certain subordinates receive prompt recognition for accomplishment. Discipline is assured by rapid up, down, and sideways communication.

5. *Be consistent in the administration of discipline.* Discipline requires steady pressure at the controls. A manager cannot be lax one day, ignoring any breach of discipline, and attempt to crack down the next. All rules must be impartially applied, and any penalties inflicted must be based on a full knowledge of the facts and in line with the gravity of the offense. However, each act requiring a penalty should be considered individually, and mitigating factors (if any) should be weighed before fixing punishment.

6. *Provide the example.* The army has the saying "You can't give orders unless you know how to take them." The same thing goes for discipline. The manager is the pacesetter and must give subordinates the example of his own disciplined performance to use as a model. He must be mentally disciplined in his planning and organization of work. He must set high standards for himself, and to get results he must manage discipline not by mood but by consistency. This kind of manager can ask the best from subordinates and get it. He asks more of himself and gives it.

2

THE FRINGE CURTAIN

The Security Package: Motivator
or Satisfier?

INSECURITY IS NOT A BUGABOO to the modern American employee as, perhaps, it was to his father, who had to fight his way through a depression. Wages are high; salaries are high; and jobs, especially for skilled people, are abundant.

During the thirties an employee knew without being told that he was in an envied position. The fact that he was working put him in a separate class, and a job itself was sufficient incentive for self-discipline. An employee had to produce in order to hold his spot on the payroll.

To be sure, there was unrest. The greatest union organizational drive in history took place after the enactment of the Wagner Act, and there were sitdown strikes, mass picketing, and violent labor disputes. But unions based their arguments for membership on higher wages and job security, and the term "fringe benefit" was still to be introduced into the lexicon of industrial relations. A laborer at one of the large automobile companies received 50 cents an hour when he began work, and if after 30 days he attained permanent status this was raised to 60 cents. There were no paid vacations and no paid holidays for hourly people.

Even if a union won bargaining rights at a company, it could not prevent layoffs when business was not sufficient to maintain employment. Management directed its efforts toward "spreading the work," and the reduced workweek was a device to which companies resorted to give as many people as possible paying jobs. Numerous employers as a matter of policy refused to hire married women, particularly if their husbands were working. A supervisor did not have to rely so much on democratic leadership to assure department discipline and high productivity. He could be reasonably sure that his orders would be carried out and that his subordinates would put in a fair day's work. The employees themselves realized that their jobs were extremely important to their security and that, when a man lost his job, he was probably in for long, frustrating weeks of searching before he could find another one.

The Fringe Push at the Bargaining Table

It was not until after World War II that paid holidays and vacations and other types of fringes became important matters of bargaining between unions and management. Consider only such fringes as holidays and vacations and how they became standard benefits for blue-collar people. Originally, unions advanced the argument that it was unfair to hourly employees to give them unpaid holidays at Thanksgiving, Christmas, and New Year's when office people were compensated for this time. "Such holidays," unions contended, "are in point of fact enforced layoffs at periods when workers can least afford them."

This argument made sense, and in the automotive industry the six-paid-holiday pattern was established, together with vacation programs. But the eligibility rules were strict. An employee did not receive holiday pay if a paid holiday came on the weekend or during his regularly scheduled vacation. Furthermore, he had to work the day before and the day after the holiday to be compensated for it. Initially, too, the eligibility requirements for vacations were strict. A worker on wages did not get a vacation until he had acquired a year's seniority, and it took five years' tenure to gain two weeks.

This pattern of vacations and holidays had become almost standard practice in industry by 1950, and pensions and insurance programs were expanded and liberalized. At present there are almost no eligibility stipulations so far as paid holidays are concerned, and employees receive them whether or not they fall on workdays. Vacations have been lengthened and eligibility requirements for them reduced almost to the vanishing point. Three- and four-week vacations for long-service personnel are generally standard practice among major companies, and certain industries grant veteran employees sabbatical leaves.

The fringe package has grown to tremendous size during the past two decades; and, in addition to holidays, vacations, pensions, and insurance programs (including protection against everything from a small accident to medical disaster), such benefits as supplemental unemployment pay, funeral leave, jury-duty pay, and retraining plans have become staple fare for the contemporary industrial worker. One nationally known company listed almost a hundred benefits and services classified as fringes—negotiated, statutory, or granted unilaterally by management—that it provided for employees, and all of them were totally paid for by the employer. While it is difficult to arrive at a precise figure on the cost of fringes, it is estimated that they range from $500 to $3,000 per year per worker, and that is in addition to wages and salaries.

Changing Views on Value of Fringe Benefits

However, fringes can no longer be regarded as employee motivators. Instead, they might better be described as "satisfiers." In order to attract capable people, a competitive company must offer wages, hours, and working conditions (and this includes fringe benefits) that persuade qualified people to apply for jobs. This means that a management must offer base compensation, fringes, and working conditions that are competitive with those of other firms in its community.

Actually, according to most present-day thinking, wages and fringes have never ranked high as factors that produce good morale and superior productivity. Provided an employee is satisfied that he is receiving fair play for his effort, his judgment of management's effectiveness is based on more positive criteria. It is quite true, of course, that employees are unhappy and restive if they think that they are being shortchanged at the pay window or that working conditions are inferior. But surveys show that, once these fundamental desires have been gratified, the cooperative discipline of an organization depends on the ability of its leadership to convince individual members of the group that the interests of both are identical. It is the degree to which the employee identifies himself with the company and takes pride in its achievements and his contribution to them that will determine the quality of morale in the organization.

In point of fact, the term "job satisfaction" may be quite misleading. Employees may be perfectly satisfied at a company, and yet its productivity and efficiency may be far below standard. A complacent employee unit may be happy with its jobs, which are not very demanding, and its leadership, which asks little of the members. Companies which have enjoyed great success for many years, and which occupy enviable positions in their industries because they have some product or service that provides them with what amounts to almost a monopoly, may be content to jog along in a placid fashion somehow or other, believing that their situation has become permanent. But the management of such a company has lost its competitive urge, and the attitude of its executives and supervisors is bound to be reflected by the employees.

A firm in this condition may operate in a climate of untroubled serenity for many years. However, if the unexpected happens and hard competition suddenly challenges the company's security, neither the leadership nor the employees will be prepared to respond decisively. Dry rot has set in, and the will to compete has been eaten away. Yet, until the crisis came along, it could not have been said that either employees or managers were dissatisfied. The simple fact was that any ambitious people the company may once have employed did not (no matter how well paid) enjoy working in such an environment and took their skills and talents elsewhere. Those who remained are content with the status quo and have declined into mediocrity without even knowing it.

New employees attracted to this kind of company are usually of the same type as those who are already working there. They are likely to prefer security and peace to competition with the chance of accomplishment if it is accompanied by the possibility of failure.

The Attraction of "Likes"

An organization attracts the kind of people it deserves. The company which emphasizes the security it offers and the generosity of its fringe-benefit program as compensation for the fact that its salary level is somewhat lower than those of more aggressive enterprises is not likely to lure highly imaginative, ambitious job candidates. It would not even know what to do with one if by some mischance he accepted a position there! On the other hand, a firm which has won a reputation as up and coming and offers a tremendous range of opportunity to the capable and talented who are eager for advancement will draw the best kind of employees. It makes no difference that its standards are high and that its job demands are exacting. Able people feel that high standards give them a chance to test their mettle and prove themselves against the best.

A famous football coach who was employed by a certain university anxious to redeem its sagging gridiron fortunes remarked after some five years on the job, "I think we have finally turned things around. Our recruiting is going better, and good players are signing up with us for grants-in-aid. But I can tell you this. It's easier to build from scratch than to rebuild a team that has lost faith in itself."

"But you could offer attractive scholarships, and your athletic dormitory is the best in the conference. With the financial support the alumni were giving you, why was it so hard to get good football players?" he was asked.

"You can't buy a football team," snapped the coach. "A national champion with a coach who is known for his ability as an instructor will attract the best players whether or not the school has a plush athletic dormitory—even if its athletic scholarships don't provide as much as they do elsewhere. The athlete who wants to excel puts that first. And he's not going to wreck his chances by playing for a chronic loser no matter what financial benefits he gets."

Positive Discipline Cannot Be Purchased

No company can buy a successful organization ready-made. All it can buy is the skills, talents, imagination, and abilities of people. High wages and salaries and a luxurious fringe-benefit program are no assurance of disciplined employee attitudes. If they are given without requiring personal responsibility and self-discipline from each individual in the group, the reverse may be true. Affluence and leisure are corrupting influences if the people who enjoy them have no worthwhile objective toward which they can direct their efforts.

Furthermore, management cannot expect gratitude or appreciation from employees for benefits or compensation to which they think they are entitled anyhow. If a company is unionized, labor officials tell union members that the real author of their high pay and fringe extras is their bargaining committee, which won these rewards from a reluctant employer who, unless pressed, would be giving them far less. If a company is nonunion, sophisticated modern employees are aware that wage and salary structures are set by competitive pressures and the fact that they may be receiving even more than their associates at organized companies may be attributable to management's desire to continue to operate a nonunion shop. After all, it is standard practice for a company attempting to defeat an organizational drive to list the benefits it provides and the amount of wages that it pays in various job categories and then compare its wages and fringes with those given by companies where the union has agreements. If such a comparison is favorable—and it usually is or management would not be making it—the company argument is, "You don't need a union. Why give up your freedom for the control of an outside party when you already have everything, and more, that it could get for you?"

This argument is quite effective, as evidenced by the increasing difficulty that unions are having in organizing manufacturing companies, and it is why they are turning their attention to municipal and institutional employees (state and city) whose pay is still quite low compared to that of industry and who, for that reason, are much more likely to listen to a union's contention that it can win them higher wages. Nevertheless, as many industrial relations experts frankly admit, their companies' wage and fringe-benefit programs are a protective shield against employee dissatisfaction and not intended as motivators at all.

A vice-president of a large steel company that has remained nonunion despite persistent efforts of the Steelworkers to organize it has observed, "We pay the highest wages in the industry, and our fringe-benefit program compares favorably with any of our competitors. We can afford it because we have greater control and greater flexibility in directing our workforce. But our wages and fringe program are simply the base of our employee relations program. We need both to attract good people. To keep them and to motivate them we must give them jobs in which they are interested, the chance to advance, recognition for their accomplishments, and a leadership which has their confidence."

Management's Growing Realism

Management's growing realism, insofar as the use of its wage and salary programs is a tool in the maintenance of sound employee relations, is shown by its communications. The approach today is more pragmatic. Alert companies go to great pains to explain to their people what fringes they receive and their value. Care is taken to show each employee the factors that have been used in evaluating his job and setting his pay rate so that he will know that he is being fairly compensated for what he does. Nor does management, by its silence, allow labor to grab the credit for employee gains. However, instead of slanting its communications so as to imply that the company is acting out of altruism, it emphasizes that good wages and fringe benefits are provided because it is a sound business principle to invest in the abilities of highly productive people so they can give their best in a challenging working environment.

That is somewhat different from the methods some companies used in the fifties in programs designed to give employees the basic facts about the American economic system. The concept was excellent, and much of the material was clearly and convincingly written. But too often the point was driven home time and time again that the employee in this country should realize how well off he was financially compared to his counterparts in other nations, particularly Russia.

From these programs employees may have gained much needed information about how our economy works and the part industry plays in making it dynamic. But the fact that they were better off than Russian workers made no great impression. They knew that anyhow. Furthermore, nobody compares himself with someone who is worse off than he is; instead, he looks at someone who is *better* off. Today there are often articles and stories in newspapers and magazines by visiting foreigners who tell us that the American Negro is better paid on the average, has a higher education, and enjoys better living conditions than the vast majority of people of Europe. But that does not diminish the Negro's discontent. He is not comparing himself with Europeans; he is looking at the standards of the white community and demanding the same for himself. Whether or not he is individually qualified by education, skill, or talent to compete in a competitive job market is another matter altogether.

People have never let reason stand in the way of emotion, and their desires are generally based on emotion. It is extremely difficult to use logic to puncture wishful thinking, and nobody can purchase future gratitude by referring to past favors. William Vaughn, president of Eastman Kodak, made a somewhat similar point when he described the objectives of his company's benefit program.

"No one can prove it, but I venture to say that the

intangible and incalculable rewards go a long way to offset the cost of the overall benefit program. The sense of job income security means that an employee can concentrate his attention on the job. Is it better to wage a tactical retreat, not conceding any new or improved benefit until the pressure for it becomes irresistible? Or is it better to exercise one's freedom of choice and planning, and treat responsibility more as an opportunity to be taken at an appropriate time, in the forward conduct of the business?"

Eastman Kodak is nonunion and offers much freedom of decision in the operation of its generous fringe-benefit program. The majority of major companies, in contrast, are unionized; and many of the fringes they have granted have been demanded by labor unions, not necessarily because the employees were insisting on any one of them but because the union's policy committee, in prebargaining sessions, included them in its list of demands. In this day of pattern bargaining, if a certain fringe is conceded by a pacemaking company it quickly finds its way into the contracts of other companies whose employees may never have even heard of that particular benefit before the union began to sell its advantages. For such reasons, strange and exotic fringes have sometimes been given to employees when the money spent on them might well have been used more profitably on improving established services.

The Shape of Fringes to Come

Since trends indicate that a rapidly improving technology will continue to produce greater and greater wealth and more and more leisure, and since there is no foreseeable diminution of government spending—which means that taxes will take a great part of each individual's income—it stands to reason that pressure for fringe benefits will increase, especially if they come tax-free.

Herman Kahn and Anthony J. Weiner of the Hudson Institute, in their book *The Year 2000* (published by Macmillan in 1967), make some startling predictions about the workweek and society in general three decades hence. So industrialists, who are always anxious to have a preview of the future, invited Mr. Weiner to speak at the Industrial Relations Institute of the National Association of Manufacturers, where he addressed himself to the future of people at work.

Mr. Weiner says that, if present trends continue, an American worker will spend on an average of four hours a day at his job in 2000 A.D. and the average per capita income will be more than $10,000. Only 2 percent of the people will be soiling their hands with manual labor on production lines. As for holidays, suffice it to say that there will be plenty.

This all sounds rosy, and you may wonder what everybody will be doing 30 years hence to bring in his $10,000 per year. "People will be lawyers, doctors, technicians, and teachers rather than shop workers," Mr. Weiner claims, "because by that time production will be so computerized and mechanized that people will be needed to punch buttons and maintain and repair the machinery which produces their abundance.

"Moreover," says Mr. Weiner, "mechanization will produce cost efficiency and lower prices. Supply and demand will have less influence on marketing because cheap energy and production requiring little labor will make narrow profit lines meaningless in an affluent society."

Mr. Weiner concludes, "Since jobs in the United States will be high-paying and probably dole existence will be comfortable, money will be less of a motivational factor for workers. Job locations will be important. Even today scientists are rushing to California in response to advertisements promising 'country-club living near our offices.' Fringe benefits, exotic vacation homes, work satisfaction, and promises of time off to further education will be incentives for skilled professionals, managers, technicians, and entrepreneurs making up tomorrow's elite wage-earner class."

Such a sybaritic existence is inviting; and perhaps, if trends continue, the year 2000 A.D. will witness all the marvels that Mr. Weiner prophesies. Indeed, some experts tell us that in the future there will be a small elite class of workers whose brains and effort will support the economy, while everybody else will be supplied with an income by the state. Already there is much serious discussion of the advantages of simply paying persons who receive welfare benefits from the government a set income—no strings attached—with which they can do as they please.

However, anyone with a long memory can recall the days when economists claimed that we had reached a permanent plateau in our economic development and that there would always be large numbers of unemployed persons whom the government would have to support by make-work. The Second World War brought an end to these auguries; and at its conclusion, instead of experiencing the return of the depression that so many had predicted, the United States began the period of its biggest expansion in history. Henry Wallace's book *57 Million Jobs,* which seemed an absurd pipe dream when it was written, quickly became an anachronism.

The Danger of Undirected Leisure

The danger of leisure without direction is that it saps people of their vitality. The Roman emperors who pacified the mobs with the fringe benefits of circuses and bread and holidays found that with each succeeding year the demand was for more.

Rome's economy was based on slave labor, which freed many Roman citizens from manual labor. But Rome in its later days was not famous for the responsibility and self-discipline of many of its citizens, and the rise in what today would be called the fringe benefit of holidays coincides with its decline. For example, during the reign of Caesar Augustus there were 76 holidays, which the people enjoyed with all the games and trimmings. By the time of Nero there were 176 of them, and Rome was well on its way downhill.

Rome maintained itself by the efficiency of its army, which constituted the elite class, and so long as it could defend the borders and keep the mobs under reasonable control the Empire was able to exist after a fashion. This suggests that, if automation frees the American citizen from work and provides him with subsidized leisure, affluence may very well destroy his society—unless he uses his time constructively. The United States has become prosperous through the pride and endeavor of its citizens. If, eventually, it becomes unnecessary for many people to work, and if the tradition of work is all but abandoned, a suitable substitute for work will have to be found that will absorb people's energies. The consequences of not finding such a substitute are easily predictable, and—to judge from existing problems and attempted solutions for them—they will not be pleasant.

But at present our concern is not with the year 2000 A.D. but with the immediate future. And contemporary management is faced with the problem of continuing to operate a disciplined and efficient workforce in an environment that is rapidly changing.

Fringe Benefits as a Positive Force

Whatever the world may be like in the year 2000, at present most Americans must find employment. Therefore, management must seek by both traditional methods and innovation to build and maintain a self-disciplined, highly motivated, productive workforce. A sound fringe-benefit program is an integral part of an equitable wage and salary structure, and it can help assure the harmonious working environment without which good employee relations are impossible. But realistic companies understand that equitable wages and fringe benefits are employee satisfiers and not motivators; and that, if intelligent, perceptive leadership is lacking, money and benefits will buy nothing at all.

If management examines its fringe program pragmatically, it should come to certain basic conclusions, which may be listed as follows.

1. Wages and fringe benefits are granted not only because of employee or union demands but in the enlightened self-interest of the company. It must have a competitive wage structure in order to attract capable job candidates.

2. In a period of high taxes and high prices, it is almost impossible for the average person to save enough out of income to maintain himself and his family in retirement or to protect them in case of prolonged sickness. There-

fore, it is natural for employees to seek such security in the form of pensions and various types of insurance.

3. The tax situation with regard to group life insurance, group health insurance, pensions, and profit sharing, combined with the efficiency of the group technique, results in greater benefits to an employee than he could provide for himself if he purchased them privately. While such plans are quite expensive to corporations, they at least receive relatively favorable treatment from the Internal Revenue Service. In other words, a dollar applied to fringe benefits will buy an employee more security than he could purchase for himself with the same dollar in a wage raise, and the company may claim tax deductions for fringes as a "necessary and reasonable business expense."

4. Any successful fringe-benefit program must have the support of employees. In short, they must want the benefits with which they are provided. Before any such benefits are given to workers, careful studies should be made of their needs; and perhaps discussions should be held, with employee leaders, even if a company has no union, before a particular fringe is established. Some companies conduct periodic attitude surveys to discover what types of benefits employees wish and use this information to help shape their fringe-benefit package. Management should do its best to tailor-make its benefit program to fit the requirements of its various employee groups, and it should try not to establish a particular fringe simply because "everybody else has it" in the mistaken notion that employees automatically want and need what everybody else has.

5. A fringe-benefit program must be carefully administered, and abuses should not be permitted. For example, employees will tend to prolong coffee breaks and wash-up

time unless supervisors win their cooperation, and occasionally discipline must be used to put a stop to such expensive practices. Firm management leadership and effective communication serve as insulation against misuse of privileges.

6. While a company cannot expect to purchase employee gratitude by giving high wages and costly fringes, it should make absolutely certain through its communication program that employees have a thorough understanding of the dollar cost of the fringes from which they benefit. This knowledge should make them more realistic in their demands, for with it they will not have the excuse of ignorance.

7. A sound wage and salary program is a shield against union organization, provided the policies and practices of a company, plus the leadership of its executives and supervisors, are fair and consistent. Even in an organized company, middle-class incomes usually produce middle-class attitudes. The well-to-do worker living in his own home in the suburbs is certainly far less likely to strike or take part in other actions that might jeopardize his property than is the employee who thinks he has little to lose. Minimal wage rates paid by municipalities to laborers, hospital workers and garbage collectors will very likely make them willing listeners to organizers who might get little attention from the employees of major manufacturing companies.

8. Management should maintain complete records of the cost of its fringe-benefit program, and its communications on this subject should stress clarity and avoid the "hard sell." An example of such an approach is found in the statement of a major manufacturer that tells employees just why the company provides fringe benefits. This state-

ment reads: "The company . . . does not 'give' its employees these things. No company can afford to give them, any more than it could afford to give away its products. Those who work for the company are entitled to them because they earn them. These job advantages, like the job itself, can be provided only by a sound business that is earning money. They are made possible by quality production, efficient operation, and hard selling—three things which can be achieved only through the combined effort of all of us."

9. A good fringe-benefit program helps create constructive working conditions and a positive climate for leadership. Employees freed from economic worry can concentrate on their jobs and consequently are more responsive to the leadership of supervisors and higher management. But it is not fringe benefits in themselves that produce high morale and disciplined productivity. These come from the ability of individual managers to win the interest, cooperation, and support of subordinates.

The Symptoms of Indifference

The president of a major American company summed up the responsibilities of a supervisor in these words: "He has his job cut out for him. He has got to make employees understand that their future rides with their contribution to organizational competitiveness and that quality is the only insurance that underwrites job security. The symptoms of noncompetitiveness are not difficult to identify. And alert management uses communications to persuade employees why it's in their interests to correct them." What are these symptoms?

1. *Waste.* Indifference and carelessness create waste. No fringe-benefit program will protect a company against it. Protection can come only from employees who understand that high costs threaten their wages, benefits, and security.

2. *Absenteeism.* Fringe benefits do not make a manager invulnerable to absenteeism. In fact, certain fringes—paid sick leave, health insurance—may even encourage it. The absent or tardy employee is a drain on company efficiency. To control attendance, every supervisor must know his people as individuals and must correct attitudes that may cause a person to stay at home. An employee who is needed on the job and who feels he is needed there is seldom absent. That is why positive communication is more effective for the majority than the penalties of discipline for missing work.

3. *A high accident rate.* Careless safety practices are costly, and training is the only means a manager has to insure that accident-free working practices are automatic with subordinates. Follow-up is also essential because, during follow-up, a supervisor can use the principles of effective communication to sell employees on the need for sensible safety rules and working habits.

4. *Too much overtime.* Overtime is sometimes necessary, but if it is due to poor planning, careless scheduling, or breakdowns in communication it is simply a sign of inefficient and expensive management. Certain of these items are controlled by the individual supervisor. Therefore, when overtime is ordered, it is wise to learn the reason why. If better planning and scheduling or more careful employee selection in work assignments would have eliminated it, the way to improvement and reduced costs is clearly marked.

5. *Failure to cooperate.* Cooperation is the key to achievement, and it must be willingly given by employees. The manager who pays attention to the ideas of his subordinates and understands their reactions knows how to build group pride, and with the members of the group cooperation is automatic. Employees pay for their wages and fringes by their productivity. Therefore, it is certainly in their interest to maintain the competitive position of their company if they wish to retain the security these benefits assure.

3

RULE BOOK
OR RULE OF REASON?

Management Ground Rules for
Positive Discipline

AMERICAN INDUSTRY HAS COME A LONG WAY since those
early days in our history when a New England manufacturer advised male employees who threatened or were insubordinate to their overseers that they risked corporal
punishment. The rules and regulations that govern em-
ployee-management relations are many and complex; they
affect every aspect of employment from recruitment and
selection to compensation. These rules are no longer established only at the discretion of the company, even if it
does not have a relationship with a union. Some are em-
bodied in law—state or federal—which, among other things,
forbids management to discriminate in hiring on the
grounds of race, creed, color, age, or national origin and

fixes minimum pay and overtime rates for companies in interstate commerce. Others are reached through the process of negotiation with a labor organization (when a union has bargaining rights with management); and, finally, still others are established by company policy.

The Concept of Self-Discipline

The rules and regulations of a modern company are designed to promote a constructive working environment, protect the health and welfare of personnel, and assure individual employees full protection from capricious or arbitrary decisions of management. Sensible rules are essential to organizational effectiveness, and if they are understood and accepted by the members of the organization as an intelligent guide to cooperative endeavor they will be supported.

It is only when regulations seem harsh, unnecessary, stupid, or unfair that there is opposition to them from the majority of people, and even then the opposition is often based on misunderstanding or misinterpretation of the intent of a rule rather than on logic and common sense. The supervisor who enforces a company rule may be asked for an explanation of the reason for it. If he then replies, "Don't ask me. I don't make the rules, I just see that they are obeyed. If you want to stay out of trouble, you'd better do what they say," he is asking for problems. The modern employee will not accept this kind of answer. He wants a reason—a reason that he believes is sound and sensible.

Since the supervisor is the day-to-day administrator of his company's rules and regulations, it is obvious that he

CARNEGIE LIBRARY
LIVINGSTONE COLLEGE
SALISBURY, N. C. 28144

requires thorough training to carry out his assignment properly. He must understand the philosophy behind each rule, he must have a precise knowledge of what is intended by it, and he must be able to give a clear and reasonable explanation for its existence if he is to make it meaningful and acceptable to employees. His key job is to create an employee climate in which rules are obeyed freely by the members of his group and are, in effect, self-enforcing because people realize they are designed to protect the employees' best interests.

When a company deals with a union, the signing of each new agreement is usually followed by a meeting at which supervisors, department heads, and other concerned executives are assembled and the contract is reviewed and discussed. Management's objective is to make sure each member of its executive and supervisory team understands the intent of every provision in the agreement, can interpret and administer it consistently and fairly, and can answer employee questions about it. Such knowledge makes every man more skillful in handling grievances and adjusting employee complaints.

The importance of communication also is stressed; thus managers and supervisors receive instruction in interviewing, in handling grievances, in administering discipline, and in giving all forms of employee training. The money that management spends on various types of supervisory and executive education runs literally into the billions of dollars each year. By and large it has paid tremendous dividends. For most supervisors will tell you the deliberate rule breaker or trouble maker is unusual in a well-run plant and that, provided proper procedures are followed and management bases its case on documented facts, not much trouble is encountered in disciplining him.

Management should constantly evaluate the necessity for each of its rules and policies relating to employee relations. When a rule or policy is out of date, it should be modernized. If it is unneeded, it should be abandoned. If it is too harsh or too severely applied, it should be modified.

Rules and policies are simply controls. And people instinctively want to live within the framework of intelligent controls. However, if controls become burdensome or annoying—and this can happen where there are too many of them—they will be resisted and not accomplish their purpose. The ideal of the rule maker or policy maker may be expressed by a paraphrase of a description of what a woman's dress should look like: "Long enough to cover the subject but short enough to attract interest." Rules and policies should be sufficient in number to cover the subject but not so many as to make employees so rule-conscious that they lose their initiative and interest in the job. Nor should employees feel that they are shut off from management by an iron curtain of regulations.

The Peril of the Punitive

A punitive approach to the matter of discipline is an admission of defeat even if it is temporarily successful. A penalty for the violation of a rule should be inflicted, not to punish an employee, but to restore him to the discipline of the group. Even if he must be dismissed, the action is aimed at removing a person who is disturbing the order of the work group and upsetting its morale. There is no thought of taking reprisal against him for the offense that he has committed.

The Western Plywood Company of Canada, in its determination to eliminate the concept of punishment from its supervisors' administration of discipline, has gone to the extreme of continuing to pay employees who have been laid off for disciplinary offenses until they are returned to their jobs. The company says the purpose of the suspension is to give the employee time to consider the results of his behavior and to judge for himself whether he wants to be a member of the team and live by its rules. It adds that time off without loss of pay provides this opportunity.

Does it work? The company thinks so. An executive claims, "Every time an employee has been sent home without pay a grievance has resulted. Under the new program, grievances seldom grow out of suspensions since no punishment is involved. The expense of grievance meetings was much greater than the cost of paying an employee for time off while he thought about his future with the company."

But There Must Be Penalties

Such a philosophy stands little chance of winning general acceptance from management, and indeed it offers considerable room for exploitation by the opportunistic or the incorrigible. Unhappily, fear of punishment is still the only deterrent to many; and, while management should stress the positive approach in the administration of rules, its determination to exercise firm discipline in the cases of persons who simply will not live by them must be implicit in its conduct of employee affairs. Permissiveness to some people is a signal for license, and rules that are applied negligently or laxly are soon ignored altogether. On the other hand, when employees support rules which they accept as sensible, these become automatic and built-in regulators of conduct, and if they are broken other employees will quickly bring the offender back into line.

"When I began work on the railroad," said the personnel director of a large railroad company, "I started in the freight yard. I was 14; and, although I knew the rule against walking on a rail, it was still fun. One day I was doing this when a big hand caught me by the seat of the britches and hauled me up on the cowcatcher of a moving engine. It belonged to a brakeman who was riding the cowcatcher, and he didn't say a word. When the engine stopped, he gave me a kick in the seat that sent me spinning. Another employee who saw what happened said, 'Now maybe you'll remember the rule about walking on a rail. If that engine had hit you that would have been the end. The reason for the rule is that a freight yard is a noisy place, and if you fall on the tracks by trying some fool stunt like that you might get killed by a locomotive you didn't even hear bearing down on you. You're lucky a foreman didn't see you.' "

Of course, it is seldom that a person has to have a rule so firmly impressed upon the seat of his trousers. But the personnel director required no further explanation regarding the practicality of the rule, and never, from that time on, did he disobey it.

If management can sell employees on the value of a rule, they will willingly accept it. If management's philosophy of discipline is positive and based on training and employee involvement in the development of rules and regulations, these will then become the framework of order and a guide to cooperative endeavor. Sound discipline is the foundation of self-control and, as such, is a motivator of high morale because it is based on the premise that good instruction and opportunity for participation make punishment unnecessary.

Any organization, from a social club to a labor union, from an athletic team to a company, must have rules to govern its operations. The exact nature of these rules will depend on the needs of the organization itself, and naturally these vary. The average company has rules controlling every aspect of employee affairs from absenteeism to wash-up time, and such regulations are generally designed to prevent abuses of benefits or privileges employees may enjoy or to protect them from accident. For example, the average person can understand why a company insists that an absent employee notify his company when he cannot report to his job (and why). And, if he fails to do so within a reasonable length of time and can present no valid excuse for his failure, no one—usually not even his union—will think management unjust if it marks him down as having voluntarily quit.

There are only two good reasons by which a manager can justify penalizing a subordinate for the infraction of a rule or the violation of a policy. They are (1) to correct a subordinate and restore him to the discipline of the group and (2) to deter other employees who might be tempted to do the same thing if an associate is allowed to get away with it. Penalties imposed for motives of reprisal, anger, or fear or in the misguided belief that being a stern and rigid disciplinarian will win respect and instant obedience are harmful because they only create opposition and disunity.

Discharge: Industry's Capital Punishment

There are certain grave offenses—such as pilferage, drunkenness, the use of narcotics while on duty, fighting, the carrying of dangerous weapons, gambling, and the like—that rate the penalty of instant discharge. Again, the reason for the severity of the penalty in cases of this kind is obvious: Persons guilty of such acts represent a threat to the safety and welfare of the organization and must be removed from it for its good.

Any company which, after a fair hearing and a careful consideration of any mitigating circumstances, finds an employee guilty of what is generally considered an offense that merits summary discharge will seldom have an arbitrator overturn its decision. In fact, the distinguished arbitrator Burton K. Turkus points out that management not only has the right to establish fair and reasonable regulations but is expected by employees to do so; and, if a company's administration of rules is equitable and consistent, it will encounter minimum trouble from either employees or union. He then lists four principles which he follows in deciding whether or not a manager has applied plant rules fairly—principles that are fundamental to the success of positive discipline.

1. *The rule must be reasonable.* What constitutes reasonableness may vary from plant to plant according to the nature of the company, the requirements of the activity, and corporate aims and legitimate interests. An employee smoking in an area where explosives are stored merits a more severe punishment than a worker who is smoking in a prohibited area where it is not dangerous.

2. *An employee must have a clear understanding of what is expected of him under the rule.* The regulation

must be publicized and explained in such a way that there is no question of the worker's understanding it perfectly.

3. *The company has the right to have a well-disciplined workforce.* This means that an employee must in good faith recognize and observe rules that are both reasonable and known.

4. *The company has the authority to administer discipline when rules are violated.* But the discipline must be reasonable and consistently applied, and "consistently" does not mean "rigidly." Management should take into account the circumstances of each case, and the gravity of the offense (not the supervisor's whim) must determine the penalty.

The Right to a Hearing

In the modern American company, a great effort has been made to assure employees full protection of their rights, to provide them with the machinery through which they may seek quick redress if any supervisor treats them unfairly or applies a rule in a discriminatory manner. In companies which deal with labor unions, this machinery is formalized and officially described as the grievance procedure. It permits an employee or a union to register a complaint and, under a procedure similar to that which would be followed in a court of law, to carry that complaint all the way up to an outside and impartial arbitrator whose decision is final and binding on both parties. Executives and supervisors have only to look at the record of arbitration cases to see how many management decisions have been reversed at such hearings because a manager applying a rule did so in an arbitrary or discriminatory way or inflicted too heavy a punishment for a particular offense.

Nonunion companies, too, are usually careful to train their supervisors and executives to administer plant rules and company policies fairly and to give considerate attention to employee complaints and problems. Such companies know full well that widespread employee dissatisfaction with what they consider management's heavy-handed application of rules or its disregard of what they believe to be their rights is an open invitation to union organization.

"Poorly trained supervisors who have played 'favorites' among employees, administered the rules as they saw fit, and failed to do their jobs as communicators and leaders have been the cause of more lost union elections than have complaints about wage and salary and benefit programs or working conditions," observes J. George Piccoli, labor relations director of the General Aniline and Film Corporation. "Many nonunion companies have established formal grievance procedures by which employees may seek justice if they think they have been unfairly treated, and although few of these procedures end in outside arbitration, the companies claim they work extremely well."

This is not surprising. After all, even at organized companies the vast majority of grievances are settled without the help of an arbitrator; and an intelligent management, motivated by nothing more than its own self-interest, will generally do its best to apply its policies equitably and correct mistakes that may have been made in their administration. Even nonunion companies which do not have formal complaint machinery are conscious of their responsibility to their workers and careful to train supervisors in the practice of good human relations, in which the fair administration of rules and policies plays an integral part.

This does not mean that American industry has reached a state of utopia in its handling of employee affairs. In large corporations the supervision of employees is divided among thousands of people, some more talented than others, and mistakes are bound to be made—mistakes of judgment and mistakes due to bad temper and undue haste. But, by and large, the American employee receives more information about the operations of his company, the reasons for its rules and policies, its financial standing, and its future plans than any other employee on earth, and this most union officials admit either privately or openly.

In fact, the International Union of Electricians (AFL-CIO) argued in effect before the National Labor Relations Board that the communications program of the General Electric Company was so successful that it undermined the union's influence with its members. The Board's decision —which many might deem a curious one—held that while no single act or piece of communication on the part of the company in itself was an unfair labor practice, all of them taken together constituted such an offense, or that the sum of the parts is greater than the whole.

The Apologists for Violence

A company cannot exist without rules of discipline which permit the constructive and positive cooperation of people working together. Fortunately, the majority of Americans want just that, including most college students. If attitude surveys are accurate, the huge majority of the latter group are not hostile to industry and to other institutions but would like to see certain reforms instituted. In that they are not very much different from generations that preceded them. It would be strange indeed if young people accepted uncritically every aspect of the establishment that their elders provided for them. These same surveys show that many college graduates plan careers in industry, and this alone would indicate that they are not anxious to destroy by anarchic acts organizations in which they hope to earn their livings.

However, the attitude and actions of the majority are overshadowed by the attitudes of the few who attempt to justify and condone violent dissent regardless of the fact that in the process of such dissent the rights of the majority may totally be disregarded.

Eric Hoffer, the longshoreman-philosopher, in discussing the breakdown of discipline in this country and the lack of concern and even contempt that some people seem to have for law and order, has observed: "It is the fashion now among educated people to feel uneasy about success —not uneasy enough to give up the fruits of success but enough to feel guilty about it and emote soulfully about the grievances of the disadvantaged and the defects and sins of the status quo. Right now it is a mark of distinction to have a sense of guilt and fashionable to confess sins."

From many of the nation's leaders you hear the argument that this country cannot secure respect for its laws until it cures its social ills. They also contend that the poverty and ignorance of the slums breed crime and that, if poverty and ignorance could be eliminated, crime would automatically disappear. This line of reasoning sounds good on the surface, but its fallacies are immediately apparent. F.B.I. reports show an alarming increase in the rate of crime among younger persons from affluent middle-class homes who have enjoyed every material advantage. And a reading of history will reveal that one of the nocturnal delights of the rich and idle young aristocratic bully boys of degenerate Rome was to form gangs and prey on ordinary citizens, committing every crime in the register from rape and robbery to murder. Yet the dean of one respected law school commented recently at an American Bar Association meeting that lawbreakers should not be prosecuted if their cause was worthy, and another speaker suggested that persons engaged in civil disobedience should be given salaries by the government for fighting unjust laws—although who would judge whether or not such laws were unjust he did not say.

Rules: The Cement of Society

It is obvious that no society could exist, and certainly no company could hope to operate successfully, if each individual had the right to obey only those rules and regulations that he considered fair and ignore all others. Nor would the average taxpayer agree that his money should go to the support of disorderly street dissenters whose views he probably not only disagrees with but deplores.

Such a permissive attitude toward disorder and such a justification of violence suggests an impracticability of leadership which is an invitation to disaster. As Judge Passmore Widgery, lord justice of the Court of Appeals in England, has pointed out, "You cannot establish an orderly society simply by curing social ills and reforming institutions." Reforms should be made where needed, and social ills should be cured so far as possible, but within the framework of reasonable rules and regulations which are accepted and supported by the majority.

Since a company is dependent for its success on the climate of the society in which it exists, management has a great responsibility to educate employees in such matters as the need for positive and meaningful rules and regulations. This was formerly not too much of a problem. The average job applicant understood it anyhow; and, when he accepted a position, he also accepted management's right to make common-sense rules to control and direct its workforce. But, with the entrance into the workforce of many persons who have neither an understanding nor an acceptance of traditional values, and of others who have rejected them, a company must give careful attention to its early employee orientation and training programs.

Protection Against Nihilism

Selection procedures should also be carefully evaluated in view of the announced plans of certain young revolutionary groups to secure jobs in industry in order to disrupt it. This is no suggestion that the selection process should be designed to keep the deserving but perhaps disadvantaged out; both society and industry will profit greatly if business plays an increasing role in making productive and useful citizens of all who are able and willing to work. It does, however, mean that a company should do whatever it legally can to protect itself from the activities of that very small minority of people who seek jobs in industry for ulterior purposes.

Any executive who reads the published plans of one student group for moving in on industry with the aim of expanding its revolt against the establishment can take no comfort from the fact that hitherto its actions have been largely confined to college campuses and that his company has been spared. It has distributed what might be described as a detailed blueprint on how a young member can procure a summer job with an employer and, after he has gotten it, exactly how he can go about enlisting support for his ideas from regular workers.

This plan cannot be brushed off as impractical or hopeless of achievement. It is an excellent guide to becoming an agent provocateur who knows how to uncover the little grievances that people think they have and, by assuming leadership in the campaign to correct them, win adherents to a cause in which those same people may not believe at all. Against this kind of infiltration industry would be well advised to strengthen its selection machinery, at least to the extent of careful investigation of job applicants' backgrounds. It should also teach its supervisors how to spot potential troublemakers and what to do about them when they are identified.

Unions will usually go along with such a program. For radical groups are no friends of traditional labor organizations; actually, union leaders are accused of "sell-out" leadership by these groups, who are just as anxious to disrupt labor as they are industry itself. In this respect, management and unions face a common foe and have everything to gain by cooperative counteraction in communication and in employee and supervisory education. George

Meany, of the AFL-CIO, has already said that "students who get jobs in industry to preach revolution may find things don't work out as they planned. Workers aren't going to be pushed around. . . ."

Industry's stake in a democratically disciplined society is as great as its interest in its own survival. A company cannot survive in anarchy. It can no more tolerate flagrant and unreasonable flouting of its own rules and regulations than it can stand by passively in the face of a nihilistic revolution. It is the responsibility of management to stand on the principle of cooperative order and oppose the temptation to take repressive right-wing counteraction against radical dissidents as sternly as it resists the actions of those few who would substitute the tyranny of the far left for the advantages of liberty. Personal freedom is retained only so long as people understand their obligations or personal responsibilities, and that is a lesson which, unfortunately, too few leaders—political or otherwise—have tried to drive home in recent years either by words or by example.

British industry has suffered so heavily from wildcat strikes that even a Labor government finally was constrained to try to take mild corrective measures. The reaction of the unions was easily foreseeable: Accustomed to having their own way, they would accept no restrictions, however bland—and this despite the fact that attitude surveys in the British Isles showed that the public was fed to the teeth with constant and needless work stoppages and that many rank-and-file union members themselves wanted something done to remedy the situation. It is a depressing fact that, if people lose their sense of responsibility and discipline, they have extreme difficulty in recapturing it.

Organized Rule Breaking

There are certain types of organized rule infractions which are beyond the power of any individual supervisor to control. For example, it is not unheard of for a union, as part of its broad strategy in bargaining, to harass a company with a flood of manufactured grievances in order to wear down management and gain certain objectives. In this case, there is little that a front-line supervisor can do except to recognize the complaints for what they are and inform those of his superiors who are responsible for union relations. Such a situation calls for top management decision. However, the more accurate and detailed the information that the decision-making executives receive, the better they can determine how to respond to it. (Further comment on his subject will come in a later chapter.)

Positive communication always breaks down unless it meets with the response of reason, and if violations of company rules are part of a campaign of planned disorder it does little good to talk to the violators about their offenses. They are depending on group action to protect them from reprisal against acts which, if committed individually, would have been met with punishment. That is why wildcat strikes, sitdown strikes, and slowdowns are so difficult to handle.

Guide Rules for Rule Making

Since rules and policies determine the operating climate of an organization, and since modern management uses them to build in employees the attitudes and behavior of self-disciplined adults, they should be based on a positive philosophy of cooperative group endeavor. Therefore, the following suggestions may be helpful to the executive or manager who seeks to make his company's policies and regulations a firm foundation on which to base enlightened employee relations.

1. *Rules and policies should be tailor-made* to reflect the actual needs of an organization and reviewed periodically to make sure that each one is still performing a useful function. Rules and policies should be changed as circumstances and conditions change, and a rule or policy should be quickly eliminated if it is no longer required. Rules or policies that are not fulfilling their original intent, or are misunderstood and resented by employees because they have been misinterpreted, wrongly applied, or found lacking in clarity or purpose, should be revised and explained. Finally, no rule or policy should be allowed to remain on the books if it is not consistently enforced. When employees are allowed to disregard one rule, they may feel inclined to disregard others.

2. Supervisors and executives should understand that *discipline in its positive sense is simply another form of self-control.* A well-trained, highly disciplined employee group is not rule-conscious. Living within the framework of regulations, the members' acceptance and understanding are automatic because they know that rules and policies are only common-sense directions for working together. If management does its training job properly, discipline in the negative or punitive meaning of the word will be a minor problem. Therefore, a far-seeing supervisor or executive will consider the infraction of a rule as an opportunity to counsel and train and not merely to punish.

3. The true test of a self-disciplined organization and the willingness of employees to accept company rules is

how well a department or work group does its job in the absence of the supervisor or executive in charge. Any manager who feels he must "police" subordinates to make sure that rules and policies are observed has failed in his job of training and in his responsibility for leadership. His very lack of trust is apparent to the employees, and where there is no trust there can be no real cooperation.

4. *Management cannot take it for granted that employees understand rules or policies* simply because they are clearly stated and posted. Supervisors and executives should explain all rules and policies governing an employee's working relationship with the company and tell him why each rule is needed. If an employee understands the need for a rule and realizes it is designed either to protect his safety or to assure the working efficiency of the group, he is likely to give it his full support.

5. When a rule has been violated, *it is a sign of weak leadership to ignore the offense simply because it is a minor one* or it is too much trouble to take action. All rules should be consistently and fairly administered. If it is necessary to impose a penalty, that penalty should be in line with the gravity of the offense; precedent, together with mitigating circumstances, should be carefully considered. The supervisor or executive should make sure that he has all the facts on a particular case and has given the employee full opportunity to defend himself. Any disciplinary interview should take place in private. The penalized employee should understand that his punishment has been imposed only after objective consideration of the case and that neither anger nor emotion has influenced the decision. He should be told that the penalty ends the incident; that, if he performs satisfactorily in the future, it will be forgotten. Actually, the imposition of a penalty provides the

experienced manager with the opportunity for constructive human relations counseling.

6. *Management should discuss policies and rules with employees and consider their suggestions* if they have merit. If employees want a particular rule eliminated and management cannot discard it, management should explain why and perhaps consider how the rule could be revised in order to gain acceptance from employees and still accomplish its purpose.

7. *No rule or policy should be applied so harshly that it works an unnecessary hardship* on anyone. In unusual circumstances, an exception can be made to almost any rule or policy without such an exception's constituting a precedent.

8. *No management can write an infallible rule book* complete with a catalog of offenses and the appropriate penalty for each. It is impossible to prepare how-to-do-it directions for every conceivable problem a manager will encounter. Besides, a heavy canopy of rules and procedures is smothering to initiative. A manager must rely on his knowledge, training, experience, and judgment in enforcing rules and making discipline decisions. Sound management programs can give him the knowledge and training he needs to do the job, and the passing years will give him experience. Judgment he must acquire for himself. If he cannot develop this quality, he should not be in a position of leadership.

9. Management should remember that *employees work best when rules are few and easily understood,* and it should rely on the positive approach to enforce them. Supervisors and executives should be inculcated in the company philosophy that discipline is a morale builder, not a punitive weapon; that thorough training is the preventive

maintenance that safeguards rules; that correction, not punishment, is the purpose of penalties; and that the manager himself creates the climax of discipline by his own leadership. If he administers the rules impartially and consistently; if he makes sure that their meaning and purpose are understood; if he is confident that his penalties are always suited to the offense and imposed objectively to correct a rule violator and deter others, not simply to punish an offender for the sake of punishment; if he is quick to recognize and credit subordinates for improvement or for good performance, then he will have little difficulty with "scoff-rules." Employees will be too busy doing their jobs to risk losing his respect by immature behavior.

Leadership Is the Key

Leadership is the key to cooperative discipline, and leadership is urgently needed at all levels of management if it is to meet the challenge of the future.

Robert Paxton, former president of General Electric, once remarked: "Our affluence, with its easy growth and expansion, has nurtured slovenliness that the economy cannot afford." He also advised that if industry is to continue to progress it must secure the understanding of government, the public, and employees regarding the realities of the times. The problem is clearly identified by Mr. Paxton, but to identify a problem is far from solving it.

The man whose capability will have a "make or break" result on his company's future employee relations program is the front-line manager—the supervisor. The morale of any athletic team stems from its confidence that it can take on and defeat all comers, and this attitude is instilled in them by the coach. The supervisor is the coach, the instructor, the boss of the working group he directs. The attitude of the group will be a reflection of his. It has often been said that a leader can see his performance mirrored in the faults of his subordinates. If he is lax, so will they be. If he lacks confidence, so will they be indecisive. If he refuses to delegate, so will employees reject personal initiative.

In the years ahead, management will put an increasingly large load on its supervisors. It should exercise great care in their selection and training. And the vital quality that each must have is the power of positive leadership.

"Leadership" is a hard word to which to give meaning, and the methods of leaders are different. But good leaders possess common characteristics. They are able to secure and retain the cooperation, trust, and support of subordinates who have confidence in their judgment and identify themselves with their interests. They also have the ability to motivate their people. Other traits they apparently share may be listed as follows:

1. *Persistence.* Leadership takes day-in, day-out stamina. The risk is great because in management the only security lies in individual competence; however, that is the best kind of security and the only kind that inspires confidence in oneself and in others. Furthermore, there is no assignment that is more rewarding than building a competitive employee organization that takes pride in its ability to face any job and push it through to completion.

2. *Job knowledge.* Formerly authority was granted on traditional grounds. The boss was boss because he owned the company. Nowadays authority is granted on the more rational basis of proven ability. More and more it will be

based on specialized competence. But leadership will always make the same demands. The supervisor who is successful in motivating employees is the one who lives up to the high standards he sets for himself. Subordinates who can satisfy a boss who expects the best from his people and will accept no less, but who has the knowledge and ability to teach them how to give it, take pride in being part of a working team that knows how to get things done.

3. *The will to accomplishment.* A successful manager thinks like a manager and has the attitudes of a manager. Possessing a belief in himself, he is willing to accept the risk of responsibility for satisfaction of accomplishment. Such a leader is proud of his subordinates and builds this same pride into their working habits and attitudes by his instruction, by his communications, and by his trust in their abilities. Employees respond to this kind of leadership, and their response is reflected in group pride and solidarity.

4. *Selflessness.* A successful leader puts the interests of the group above the desires or ambitions of any one person in it. He does not seek easy popularity by laxness or soft compromise. Personally self-disciplined, he constantly shows his willingness to face responsibility even when the challenges are hard and the danger of failure is great. When he accepted a position of leadership, he recognized its cost. He understands that authority cannot be successfully exercised by the temporizer or the buck passer and that accomplishment is never reached by the road of least resistance.

4

THE THIRD FORCE

Positive Discipline and Organized Labor

ORGANIZED LABOR complicates management's administration of discipline. A union's mere existence formalizes the relationship between the company and its employees, and rules and procedures are negotiated in the union agreement which management must observe in dealing with its people. If a company has no union, it can make policy unilaterally so long as that policy is consistent with state and federal law.

The problem of discipline in a nonunion company is usually a matter for the manager and the individual employee, and it is handled on that basis. The manager can explain the reasons for his decisions privately to the employee; he need not fear action from the union aimed at forcing him to reverse his decision or at making him justify it in a formal grievance hearing. In contrast, the pressure applied by a third party acting as an advocate for an aggrieved person can make the administration of discipline and of employee relations quite difficult and extremely technical.

The Protection of Proper Procedure

This does not imply that a management loses its right to direct and control its workforce or to administer employee relations because of the presence of a union. Unionization simply obligates a company to observe the rules and procedures in the conduct of employee affairs to which it has agreed in the union contract.

Essentially, regulations governing management-employee relations are not unlike certain aspects of this nation's legal system which are intended to protect the rights of the individual and which are based on the premise that a man is innocent until he is proved guilty. For example, the purpose of the formal grievance procedure which ends in binding impartial arbitration is to guarantee the employee full protection from arbitrary or discriminatory acts of management and to make certain that he is not penalized for an offense until he has had a fair and full hearing. Such a method obviously places the stress on procedure. A manager cannot necessarily punish an employee because he is reasonably, or even absolutely, sure that the employee deserves the punishment. He must be able to prove his case.

Moreover, if in the administration of discipline the manager neglects to follow the rules established by the contract or short-cuts any of its steps, his decision may be overruled by an arbitrator. The employee will then be freed from the penalty even though there is no argument about his guilt.

All one has to do is to read reports of arbitration decisions to find examples of employees who have been caught red-handed in violations of company rules but have nevertheless had to be exonerated by the arbitrators on technical grounds, occasionally quite trifling ones.

For example, in one chemical company the smoking rule calling for immediate discharge if violated was rigidly applied because of the obvious danger. An employee was accordingly terminated by a supervisor who had seen him smoking a cigarette. Prior to the incident, other workers —afraid they would be blown sky-high—had reported the man's disregard of the rules to their boss, and the supervisor had not only warned the offender but told him that if he were caught smoking he would be dismissed. Shortly afterward, the employee was seen by the supervisor in the act of throwing away a lighted cigarette and stamping it out, and he was given the penalty the rules prescribed.

The case finally went to arbitration, where it was ruled that since the supervisor had observed the employee, not actually smoking, but only throwing away a lighted cigarette, it could not be proved that he had actually broken the rule. So the offender was reinstated—much to the chagrin of management and many of his fellow employees.

Some arbitrators are inclined to be lenient in discharge cases. If there are any extenuating circumstances, even minor technicalities, they tend to modify the punishment. In this they have taken their lead from the courts themselves. Recent rulings of the Supreme Court have caused much criticism because, in the effort to protect the rights of law-breakers, some people think the right of society to the protection of its safety has been ignored.

To be sure, discharge—as industry's capital punishment—should never be inflicted lightly. Moreover, it is absolutely necessary to safeguard personal rights, and protection of these rights marks the difference between a free democratic government and a totalitarian state. But prosecuting attorneys have lost many arguments because sharp-eyed defense counselors have noticed either technical errors made by law-enforcement officers in procedures or rights to which morally guilty defendants have been entitled but which have been denied them. As a result, the culprits have gone scot-free. Similarly, almost any veteran line manager can tell you from personal experience how he has been forced to reverse a penalty he has imposed on an employee who richly deserved it simply because he forgot to follow all of the contract procedures in handling the case.

Still, the fact that it is necessary to observe established procedures is no reason why an experienced manager cannot enforce discipline, nor does it reduce in any way his authority over his subordinates. It simply forces him to recognize that there are no short cuts to justice and obliges him to spend time and energy assembling evidence that will stand up under close scrutiny before he inflicts a punishment. It also means that he must have a sound knowledge of the provisions of his union agreement, understand the rules and regulations that govern the application of discipline, and adhere to them in his supervision of employees.

It is true that an employee may occasionally escape punishment by worming his way through a procedural loophole. But, in spite of the deficiencies in the American system of industrial justice, they are minor if it is kept in mind that orderly procedure and the right to a fair hearing constitute a solid defense against arbitrary, whimsical, or "kangaroo court" justice and a source of strength to industry itself.

The very fact that employees know they have access to impartial justice and rights that cannot be summarily abridged tends to insure their allegiance to the American system of private initiative. The modern employee in shop or office is better educated, better informed, and better paid than were his predecessors. He may not be entirely satisfied with the system or the establishment. But at least he knows how he stands vis-à-vis his counterparts in other countries; and to protect his own interests, including his property and his standard of living, he supports the system which provides these things. He may want a larger share of the "take," but this is a far cry from wanting to destroy the organization itself.

The Administration of Punitive Discipline

There is nothing strange or mysterious about the administration of discipline in a company that has contractual relations with a union although, it must be admitted, the process is time-consuming and requires knowledge, judgment, and skill. Lawrence A. Appley, long president and now board chairman of the American Management Association, has often advised executives that "meticulous attention to detail" is all-important in the execution of their duties. Certainly meticulous attention to detail, plus the consistent observance of well-established procedures, is the key to enlightened employee relations and positive discipline in an organized company.

The following rules should be the guidelines for any

manager when he is forced for the good of his working group to apply punitive discipline, whether to force an offender to cease interfering with the order of the organization or to dismiss him from it because he cannot live according to its rules and policies.

1. When an employee is disciplined, a manager should—
   a. Make certain the penalty is exactly in line with the gravity of the offense.
   b. Study the union agreement to make sure that the employee has been properly notified and that procedure (including notification of the union if necessary) has been carefully observed.
   c. Never rescind and later reimpose the suspension of an employee because evidence, not available at the time of the hearing is afterward discovered, especially if the original failure to find such evidence was due to the haste and inadequacy of the investigation.
2. In the conduct of an investigation, a manager should—
   a. Always remember that it is a fact-finding procedure and not a criminal trial.
   b. Obtain full information on such questions as who? what? when? where? why? and how? before he makes a decision.
   c. Be sure the union and the employee have been notified, as prescribed by the agreement, and that the employee's right to representation is carefully respected.
   d. Keep accurate records, including any necessary affidavits or statements from witnesses. Such com-

mon-sense precautions are essential. Witnesses sometimes change or alter oral statements, particularly if they must face hostile pressure from associates or friends. A witness has the right to read any statement he has signed and must be given the opportunity to do so. He also is entitled to retain a copy of it.

3. When holding a hearing, a manager should—

a. Make sure that it is impartial and that the employee is provided with every chance to tell his story and to give any facts that might prove his innocence or at least mitigate his offense.

b. Be certain the charge against the offender is accurate and specific. Reference should be made to the rule or contract provision which he has violated.

c. Be careful not to use an employee's past disciplinary record cumulatively against him because of his present offense unless prior offenses are pertinent and related to the one with which he is now charged. These should never be taken into account if they took place so far in the distant past that they would be rendered void by any reasonable statute of limitations. However, if they are pertinent they should be noted in the record and considered in assessing the penalty.

d. Keep in mind that an employee or his representative has the right to question witnesses who have testified against him in the same way that management is privileged to question his witnesses.

e. Remember that information or facts (no matter how valid) not presented at the hearing and unknown to the employee cannot be used in determining his punishment.

4. When an employee is disciplined, a manager should—

   a. Thoughtfully consider his past record and, if it is a good one, give this weight in fixing the penalty.

   b. Review the prior discipline record of the employee. If his past offenses are related to the present one, they should become a factor in deciding the extent of his punishment.

   c. Be extremely careful to make sure that the penalty exacted could not be considered excessive by any reasonable person. W. S. Gilbert's advice, "Make the punishment fit the crime," is the guiding rule for the wise manager; and even then, if the record of an offender entitles him to consideration, the penalty should be tempered with mercy.

   d. Remember that any discipline case, especially one involving discharge, may finally be heard by an arbitrator. If so, the burden of proof is squarely on management. It must demonstrate that there was just cause for its action. If an executive or supervisor is confident that he can clearly show just cause and has followed contract procedures, he need have little fear that the average arbitrator will overturn his decision.

   e. Avoid what is known in the legal profession as "double jeopardy." The first penalty is all that counts. It cannot be increased because further information has revealed that the offense was more serious than was originally thought, nor can an employee be charged and punished twice for the same offense even though additional facts about the case indicate that the first penalty was too lenient.

The Manager Needs Judgment and Skill

These suggestions are intended to help administer discipline in its negative or punitive sense. Fortunately, a manager who is fulfilling his full responsibilities—and that includes providing the kind of leadership to which employees respond positively—it not forced to act as a policeman or an enforcer of company rules. Subordinates will have their complaints, their problems, and their questions; but, if the supervisor is available and genuinely interested, these can usually be answered satisfactorily and individually. The average employee is not seeking to make a formal grievance out of every minor irritant. Most people have to be pushed hard before they make an official case out of a complaint even if they have grounds to do so. The time and effort it takes are too much trouble. They do not like to be centers of controversy and may even fear the consequences of raising an issue. The majority of employees want to respect and get along with their boss, and they also hope to earn his respect and confidence.

The "shop lawyer," or the man with the chip on his shoulder, is rare. True, there is somebody in almost every large group who may fit this description. If he has leadership abilities, he may be dangerous; but usually he does not exert much influence. Although he may get under the skin of his supervisor, his fellow employees probably look on him with mixed emotions. While they may have a sneaking admiration for the fellow who defies authority and speaks his piece to the boss, unless there is a pervading spirit of unrest in the organization they normally do not care to be identified too closely with him. The company can still grant or withhold many privileges and opportunities; the employee who is automatically opposed to management and strives to harass its representatives on every possible occasion is seldom marked for advancement even though the power of the union to which he belongs may make him almost immune to reprisal.

The real key to positive employee discipline is a manager's skill in administering the union agreement. A distinguished U.S. senator once remarked about a certain bill that he and his committee were considering, "I don't see why we go to the trouble of writing this legislation. We should simply ask the experts in the department to write what they want. After all, they are going to interpret the law and administer it. How they interpret it may be quite different from what we want no matter how clearly we try to state our intentions."

A long-standing criticism of the Supreme Court (and one not limited to its recent membership) has been that "the Constitution of the United States means whatever nine justices say it means." Echoing this thought is the comment of John Jones, vice-president of industrial relations for the Koppers Company, who said, "It's not what the contract says that counts, but what line management—the supervisor—thinks it says. The experts may negotiate the agreement, but the supervisor administers it. The best contract possible will do little good if it is poorly administered. The supervisor's decisions in applying the terms of the agreement may become practice. He interprets management's intent by his everyday actions. Therefore, it is vital for each supervisor to have an exact understanding of the meaning of each contract clause. This knowledge assures consistency in union-management relations, and consistency is just another way of saying good administration."

The line manager, unless he is in a key company position, is heavily restricted in his exercise of authority. His major decisions probably have to be approved by his superiors. But it is absolutely impossible for any group of top executives to write an answer book on every conceivable situation that might arise in employee-union-management relations which its executives and supervisors could use as a ready-reference guide. A company must depend on the training it gives its leadership people and on their knowledge, courage, and judgment, to assure consistently fair administration of its union agreement and its rules and policies.

A union agreement simply furnishes an outline which managers must follow in the conduct of employee affairs. There are not many specific directions on what to do in specific situations, nor can there be. Words themselves mean different things to different people. If one manager thinks a particular clause should be interpreted in one way, while a colleague in another department believes it should be interpreted in another, by acting on their beliefs without checking with someone able to provide the correct interpretation they may begin a pattern of confusion which can be extremely harmful to company discipline.

If several managers establish an inconsistent pattern of action in the interpretation and administration of various provisions of a union agreement—and this may happen before the company discovers it—the unhappy precedents that are thereby set may be extremely difficult to eliminate. In arbitration cases the arbitrator assumes that "it's deeds, not words, that count"; regardless of what a contract clause may say, he will ignore it if it can be shown that the management of the company did not observe its own rules. For example, suppose it is permissible under an agreement for a company to enforce a ten-minute coffee break but supervisors are lax and allow their people to extend this period to fifteen minutes. Then a particular supervisor, suddenly and without warning, cracks down and penalizes offenders. In this case, an arbitrator may well rule, "The employees deserve no punishment. If you did not enforce the rule as you had every right to do, you cannot now arbitrarily and suddenly apply it. Such action is discriminatory."

The union always takes the offensive in grievance matters, which automatically places the company and the manager concerned on the defensive. The manager must justify his actions; and any mistakes he has made, even if they are unintentional or purely technical (like failure to observe exact procedure as described in the contract), may give the steward a victory and an employee a settlement that may set an unhappy precedent. That is why supervisors cannot afford to make hasty or faulty decisions in labor relations. The company's program of positive discipline may be completely undermined.

Supervisors Must Be Trained

It is the obligation of responsible management to make certain that its managers receive the labor relations training they require to handle employee relations under the terms of the union contract. This does not mean that every line executive and supervisor must be an expert in labor law or in industrial relations. However, all of them should have an intelligent grasp of the subject, be able to identify potential problems when they see them, and also be aware of their long-range consequences. Such an awareness gives the manager a sensitivity in union matters. While his initiative and power of decision are in no way impeded, he knows when he needs expert advice, and he seeks such help before he takes action.

Since the danger spots in the administration of a union contract are most likely to appear when a manager endeavors to turn general directions into specific action, it is well to know those areas in which he is likely to be confronted with his touchiest problems. They are:

1. The adjustment of grievances, especially those resulting from the imposition of discipline.
2. Overtime distribution.
3. Work assignments, particularly if the union or the employees have different ideas on who should receive these.
4. The factors of ability and seniority in promotion and downgrading, both of which a manager may have the right under the contract to consider in deciding who is best qualified for a given position.
5. Changes in work assignments or employee transfers.

In each of these situations personal judgment comes into play, and consistency in management action is essential to sound employee discipline.

Since firmness and a sure touch are the key to efficient contract administration, the following checklist may be useful to any manager who wishes to be certain that his employee-relations decisions are in accord with the union agreement and consistent with the policies and precedents of his company.

1. *Be sure the grievance is accurately identified.* A manager must fully understand the employee's complaint to know whether it is actually a grievance, or simply an expression of personal discontent which has no official standing but should be heard out of sympathy, if nothing else. He can then tell his subordinate in clear, simple language what can be done about it. If there is an actual grievance on which the manager knows he must rule unfavorably, he has the opportunity to explain why. If an adjustment can be made, he has the power to make it. And if the employee simply has a personal complaint, and not a true grievance, perhaps a sympathetic hearing will do much to improve the situation.

2. *Base the decision on facts.* Impetuousness and haste often lead to mistakes in judgment. Get all the information available before acting in any situation that involves employee discipline, a grievance, or an unusual request; then be certain that you do not make commitments that could later be expensive to the organization. Nor should a decision ever be based on hearsay evidence or on surface appearances. Investigate carefully; make sure you check out all sides of a story with an objective mind before you reach any conclusion.

3. *Maintain sound records.* Records are essential to effective administration. Actions of the past become precedents, and memory is a faulty guide to what has been done before. Good records permit you to base decisions on sound precedents and provide you with the factual evidence you may later require to justify past decisions or actions.

4. *Settle grievances promptly.* Speed is the key to efficient grievance handling. If employee grievances are allowed to pile up unsettled, other grievances—or even strikes—may result because workers are unhappy over their inability to get answers from management and believe they are getting the run-around. Of course, speed should never be substituted for sound solutions; an employee understands it takes a reasonable length of time to check out the facts in an involved complaint. But he also can recognize procrastination and delaying tactics. The wise manager works on the principle that a subordinate has the right to get a decision on a complaint or an answer to a legitimate question as quickly as the information needed to give it can be obtained.

5. *Depend on honesty.* Soft answers may turn away wrath, but appeasement, sugar-coated half-promises that cannot be carried out, and disregard for company policy in the false hope of getting along with a demanding shop steward or a hard-case employee are certain ways to destroy employee discipline and morale. Every employee grievance should be settled on a fair and equitable basis as quickly as possible. Politics should not enter the picture. A manager is lost if he tries to trade grievances with a shop steward or permits personalities to influence his judgment in their settlement.

6. *Develop an effective communication system.* Keep your superior informed as to important decisions or actions that you have taken, particularly in situations that appear unusual. If management knows what you are doing, errors and mistakes in judgment can be corrected before harm results. Employees also should be provided with all the information they require for a full under-

standing of the reasons for your ruling. If a supervisor must deny an employee's grievance or cannot grant his request, the employee should be told exactly why in a sensible and convincing manner. Then he is more likely to accept the decision in good humor.

7. *Be accurate in writing replies to written grievances.* Mistakes can be costly if a reply to a written grievance is hastily prepared or contains commitments, real or implied, that cannot be fulfilled. The experienced manager makes certain that he restricts his answer to the exact complaint of the employee, but this he covers clearly in all the necessary detail.

8. *Accept full responsibility.* A manager in an organized company who directs union employees must know the union agreement, be able to interpret its provisions properly, and apply its terms consistently. For such a contract is, in reality, negotiated company policy that controls employee affairs. The manager is bound to encounter problems that he cannot solve, but it is impossible for him to improvise in the administration of a union contract or in day-to-day employee relations without creating difficulties whose effects may be far-reaching. A manager who is not technically proficient and attempts to muddle through will soon find that he is hopelessly and helplessly tangled. Even worse, the same thing will have happened to his company's employee relations program.

The Role of the Shop Steward

If management expects to administer discipline fairly and positively in an organized company, each of its executives and supervisors must have a perceptive understanding of the role and function, not only of the union, but of its plant representative—the shop steward.

In the matter of grievances, labor has defined its point of view and stand in strong, clear words: "We assert ourselves as a group to modify management's unaccountable authority." This is a rather heavy-handed way of saying that the union, through the agreement it holds with a company, can force management to account for its decisions in the direction and control of its workforce. The steward is the union's representative. It is his responsibility to demonstrate to the rank-and-file members that they are getting value in services for their dues. This he does by becoming their spokesman on issues—such as wages, hours, and working conditions—over which there is disagreement between the company and its people. Naturally, too, he represents individual employees when they have complaints, real or fancied, about some decision or action of a supervisor which has affected them adversely.

To a steward, a grievance is an opportunity to demonstrate his ability as an employee representative and to show members they are buying value for their dues money. If there were never any arguments or disputes between the company and the union, or between the company and its employees, there would be no need for a shop steward. It is easy to understand why he sometimes presses hard on minor points and appears to search for grievances, sometimes even seeming to stir them up himself, in order to make his presence felt. He has a political job, and if he relaxed and "made things easy for the boss" he would be accused of selling out to the company.

However, the average hard-working steward does not have to seek out grievances or manufacture them. Employees provide him with enough complaints to keep him busy; besides, he does not want to go too far with a case he has no chance of winning. If he is realistic, he understands that his performance is measured by his success. If his batting average is too low, he may not get reelected—and this is a possibility that certainly has considerable influence on his actions. Any manager who finds that he is constantly having to discuss phony grievances with a steward should know immediately that there is an underlying reason for the trouble. The sooner he is able to identify it, the better chance he has of restoring normality to employee relations.

Because it is essential that shop stewards have a thorough grounding in grievance handling, most unions give them intensive training in the subject. A large CIO union tells its stewards: "Study each grievance carefully to see whether you have an argument that will stand up," and provides this how-to-do-it-guide. "Ask three questions: (1) Has the contract been violated? (2) Has the company acted unfairly? (3) Has the employee's health or safety been put in danger?

"If the answer to any one of these questions is yes, you have a legitimate grievance. If it's no to all three, you probably won't win your case. In that event try diplomatically to persuade the employee not to press his gripe. But do so in a way that makes him think the decision was his own idea. You don't want him to think you are unwilling to represent him."

Here is a set of instructions taken from a union training course in grievance handling. It instructs stewards, "Write the grievance plainly and write it just as the employee gives it to you. Make sure your written grievance answers the important questions: who? what? when?

where? and why? Check it out against past grievances, past arbitration cases. Keep a good file.

"Be a thorough investigator and base your case on precedent. When you present an argument, build it on the . . . provision of the contract that covers the problem. If the contract is 'silent' on the specific matter at hand, find the provision that most nearly applies. Find a prior grievance or grievances of a similar nature that have been settled in favor of the employee. Get facts showing that the request of the employee which the company has denied has been granted in the case of other employees. This is evidence of discrimination. Get previous decisions in these similar disputes."

It does not take much imagination to see what would happen to a supervisor who attempted to play a grievance hearing by ear if he were confronted by such a well-prepared adversary. Management must do its homework equally well. But the individual manager has this assurance—he made all the original decisions. If they have been consistent with sound labor relations practices, then he can generally work out a satisfactory solution.

The shop steward may want the supervisor to do just that. He may know full well that he does not have a true case, but in his capacity as advocate for the plaintiff he has to put forth the best argument he can. If the supervisor can show the employee that his argument has no substantial merit, the employee may be satisfied to see his complaint denied. Nor will he feel the steward has let him down—after all, the fellow made every effort to win the case. Moreover, the employee and the steward will have a greater respect for the supervisor whose clear and logical explanation has shown that management's action was in line with the contract and in no way discriminatory.

A Management Guide to Positive
Grievance Handling

Skilled handling of grievances is absolutely essential to the maintenance of discipline in a modern industrial enterprise and the foundation of a positive, enlightened discipline program. The following suggestions may be useful to management and its line supervisors in the conduct of grievance discussions with in-plant union representatives.

1. *Focus your attention on the key argument.* Isolate the actual grievance and the argument that supports it. Never allow the discussion to stray off its main course. Diversionary tactics are natural, particularly for someone who does not have a good case. A manager who permits a steward to use this device successfully may become so confused that he loses sight of his own objective in a welter of extraneous and irrelevant arguments.

2. *Do not resort to delaying tactics.* An unsettled grievance is a source of danger. The longer it remains unanswered, the greater the chance of harmful results as both the grievant and the steward become increasingly frustrated and angry. Emotion always makes reasonable solutions harder to achieve. But, in striving for speed, sound investigation and thorough preparation should not be neglected.

3. *Do not threaten or bluff.* Sound discipline is rooted in the integrity and honesty of management. A manager should never threaten an action he is not prepared to take or attempt by a show of temper to frighten a steward into retreat. An experienced steward does not "scare." If he can force a supervisor into losing his head, he may well win his case even if it is a poor one. Besides, a manager whose hasty or ill-judged decisions must be reversed by

superiors is undermining his own authority and the respect employees have for him.

4. *Listen attentively.* Give the steward full opportunity to talk and encourage the grievant to do so. The more a person talks, the more likely he is to bring the truth to light. A wise manager can sometimes sit back and encourage a steward to talk himself out of his grievance.

5. *Be prepared to justify your decisions.* The ancient industrial relations maxim, "Management has the right to manage; the employee (or union) has the right to grieve," still holds true. The burden of proof is on the company. Maintain good records and base your arguments on facts, precedents, and past interpretation of the agreement.

6. *Expect the steward to profit by your errors.* The steward's reputation, so far as the employees are concerned, is based on "What have you done for me lately?" He is out to win. If you make mistakes and he takes advantage of them, do not think he is unethical or unfair. His interest is in his constituent and not in objective justice.

7. *Settle a grievance at the first stage.* The skilled supervisor settles the majority of grievances that come up at the first step of the procedure. If he abdicates his authority and simply funnels all such complaints to higher management, he has proved that he has no real authority or lacks confidence in his ability to make proper decisions. Either way, such a manager will not be an asset in a positive discipline program. Higher management should never be used as a prop; its responsibility is to adjust major or complex disputes. Minor or routine complaints that can be settled by the supervisor in charge should be settled by him; otherwise the entire discipline program will break down because top management has become too involved in petty details.

8. *Present a solid front.* In a grievance hearing, management representatives must present a united front. Any private disagreements they may have must be settled privately. If a management spokesman at a grievance meeting notices differences of opinion arising among his group, he should quickly call a recess to deal with them.

9. *Be objective.* Keep a sense of humor and remember that unions are political and politics is a hard game. Do not be thrown off stride if the steward resorts to "personalities" or uses abusive language in referring to the company or to individuals in the company. There probably is nothing personal in this behavior. He may simply be trying to goad you into anger because he knows from experience that an ill-considered statement on your part will give him his best chance of winning his case. However strong the temptation, do not permit him to trap you into replying in the same kind of language.

10. *Remember that the steward's interests lie with his membership.* As the union's in-plant officer, it is up to the steward to make the organization strong, aggressive, and able to produce results. He must earn the support of employees, and to do this he must play a role in influencing their thinking. It is his responsibility to fight hard to secure advantageous settlements for all group or personal complaints and to investigate all matters that affect employee working conditions. In the execution of these responsibilities, he will certainly cause difficulties for management and for individual supervisors. But the shop steward is here to stay, and the fact that he is around is in some ways beneficial to management. His very presence has made supervisors and executives better leaders. They have to be to do their jobs.

5

THE NEGATIVE SYNDROME

Absenteeism, Lateness, and Labor
Turnover: Symptoms of
Deteriorating Discipline

ABSENTEEISM, LATENESS, AND LABOR TURNOVER are related
problems, and in a broad sense they might be described as
symptoms indicating disciplinary difficulties within an organization. They are, however, only a surface reflection of
internal trouble and a mirrored reflection at that.

Statistics May Be Misleading

Statistics showing a high absence or tardiness rate are
not too important in themselves. Before management puts
any faith in them, the data should be analyzed carefully
to discover how many people are involved; what their

reasons have been for reporting late or not at all; what departments and job classifications are most affected; and what can be determined about the age, seniority, and sex of those employees who are prone to absenteeism and lack of punctuality. When management has secured satisfactory answers to these questions, it will be in a position to get at the root cause of its dilemma and take remedial measures.

So far as labor turnover is concerned, statistics again may be unreliable. The company that hires a number of young female clerks and typists expects a high labor turnover and takes it as a matter of course. The girls find better jobs or get married and leave work to raise families. Airlines, for instance, know there will be an almost 100 percent turnover among their stewardesses over any five-year span. The problem is not a sign of negative discipline but an indication of the exceptional desirability of the stewardesses in the marriage market. The airlines have solved the problem by conducting intensive recruitment and training programs that feed new stewardesses into their organizations as fast as they are needed; thus they have turned what might be considered a liability into an asset. Many young girls are attracted to the air-hostess career because it is glamorous, gives them a chance to travel, and usually ends up at the altar—all in the space of a few short years.

There are many companies which have similarly turned their high turnover rates among young executives into an advantage so far as recruitment and positive discipline are concerned. A vice-president of a leading textile firm once remarked, "We frankly tell potential management trainees, 'Not all of you will rise to the top of our organization. There is only room for so many. But we will give each of you a chance to learn your profession in a company that is a leader in its field. The knowledge and skills that you will acquire here will make you highly valuable to other companies at good salaries; so, if you don't make it with us, we can give you a start that will assure your careers.' This approach works. You don't have to offer security to the ambitious, only opportunity."

Sometimes there are understandably good reasons for absenteeism. "Absence without leave" has plagued American armies throughout history, but the absentees were not necessarily deserters or shirkers. In the early history of this country, the population was largely agricultural; farmers with crops and families to worry about, men who were paid small amounts of money irregularly or not at all, would frequently leave the army after a campaign on their own initiative to dig their potatoes, say, and return in time for the next battle. Generals understood that economics and not lack of patriotism caused the high rate of army absenteeism and, for the most part, accepted the situation realistically.

Yet the fact is that absenteeism, lateness, and labor turnover are not always signs of a decline in employee morale; even though there are, at times, logical and satisfactory reasons for them, they are, generally speaking, part of what might be described as the negative discipline syndrome. Employees who are unhappy, who are dissatisfied with their pay, with working conditions, with company policies, or with their leadership, will strike back with whatever weapons are available to them. Absenteeism, lateness, labor turnover, insubordination, wildcat strikes, slowdowns, and work stoppages are all methods they utilize to protest against situations or actions of management which they resent. They are flashing a red warning signal to the company that positive discipline has disintegrated and that corrective measures are immediately necessary to restore it.

Since we are concerned in this chapter specifically with absenteeism, tardiness, and labor turnover, let us take up these subjects separately and in that order.

1

Absenteeism: The Costs

Aside from the question of discipline, excessive absenteeism is extremely expensive to American business. It has been estimated by various management organizations that the cost of away-from-work employees comes to more than $7 billion annually. Some years ago the General Electric Company calculated that every dollar the absent employee did not get in his paycheck cost the company as much as $2 in its extemporized effort to continue production without him. This would include such items as training, transfers, overtime, lost production due to delays, waste, and the like.

Even under the best of conditions there will be a certain amount of absenteeism. People get sick, they must attend to private business, they go on vacations, and they are trapped at home by bad weather. But in view of the high cost of absenteeism it is self-evident that any intelligent management will make every effort to encourage full attendance from its workforce so far as that is possible.

The key to any successful absenteeism-control program lies not so much in rules as in the leadership of front-line managers. They establish a company's working climate and set the tone of discipline. They must know how to motivate, for a system of rigidly applied punishments designed to enforce attendance would probably do more harm than good. In a company that does not have a union, such a harsh approach would undoubtedly lead to its organization, for workers would seek protection through group unity. Even if this did not occur, the company's labor turnover, in a job market which offers abundant opportunity to skilled or even semiskilled men and women, would certainly soar to excessive heights, and the reputation the employer would win for himself would make it difficult for him to attract replacements. In a union company, the grievances and labor troubles that would be the inevitable consequences of arbitrary rules enforcement would make the effort hopeless.

This does not mean that chronic offenders against attendance rules should not be disciplined, even to the extent of dismissal. It is simply a realistic suggestion that absenteeism control must be attained by positive methods that win employee support and cooperation. People who are interested in their jobs, who have pride in belonging to a productive team, who believe that their individual work is important and understand that the contribution they are making to the group effort is valuable, do not stay home if they can possibly help it. On the other hand, employees who have monotonous jobs, who think it makes little difference one way or the other whether they miss a day at the plant, and who reason, "After all, when I don't work, I don't get paid for it; so why should the boss worry?" are more likely to take unpaid holidays for what would be considered frivolous or whimsical reasons.

A plant manager at an assembly operation in a little North Carolina town tucked high in the mountains put it this way: "The majority of our workers are women, mostly young girls. They earn what they consider good money; in fact, until we came here, there were few job opportunities at all. But there is no gainsaying the fact that the work is monotonous and tiring. The girls are assemblers, and the job requires that they stand up a large part of the day. When they get their paychecks, they usually have a good deal left over from what they give their families. So, when they have dates or want to go to the city to shop, they just 'take off.' It's hard for them to understand that their absences make any difference to us. They want to have a good time and enjoy their money. When they are here, they perform well and productivity is high. The trouble is they miss too much, and we are having a tough time trying to change their attitudes."

What the Record Shows

Before considering the problem of absenteeism-prone employees and what to do about them, it might be well to review certain general facts about absenteeism itself in order to understand the subject more clearly. Such an understanding will enable management to develop realistic programs for its control. Naturally, any general statement admits many exceptions; but, by and large, experts who have studied the patterns of absenteeism exhaustively know a great deal about it.

1. *Employees of large firms are likely to miss work more often* than do people working in small companies. The reason is that there is sometimes a feeling of anonymity and loss of individuality among employees in big companies. Besides, if you are a member of a large group, you are inclined to think your absence will not be missed.

2. *Women, especially younger women, have a higher absence rate* than do men. Women have greater personal family responsibilities than men, and they are also subject to physical problems that occasionally induce absenteeism.

3. *Companies that provide paid sick leave have higher rates of absence* than companies which do not. People are more likely to pamper minor illnesses by staying at home if they can do so without suffering economically.

4. *Employees who have an unsatisfactory attendance record during their first year on the job are likely to continue to be absenteeism-prone.* It is hard to get the leopard to change its spots.

5. *Employees are absent more in the shop and on assembly jobs* than in the office. Plant jobs are likely to be more monotonous and fatiguing. Moreover, plant employees, especially in unionized companies, are treated on a group basis; the individual, intimate touch is sometimes lacking.

6. *Bad weather results in bad attendance records.* Nobody likes to go to work in a snowstorm, and bed is best in a blizzard.

7. *Distance to the job is a factor* in the absence rate. If transportation is difficult and destination distant, it stands to reason that an employee's attendance rate will be affected. This problem should certainly be considered in selection.

8. *Absenteeism reaches a peak on Mondays and gives the least trouble on Wednesdays and Thursdays.* It is also likely to be high the day before and the day after a holiday. Everybody likes a long weekend, and the holiday stretch-out has become so prevalent that management has made adjustments in its working practices to try to solve the problem. Many companies now schedule holidays on

Fridays or Mondays, regardless of the calendar date on which they fall, to provide three-day weekends.

9. *Sickness (or alleged sickness) accounts for most absenteeism.* Bad colds or related illnesses are the most dangerous foes of good attendance records. Sickness cannot be avoided, and the absenteeism-prone employee is most likely to use sickness as an excuse for missing work because he knows it is difficult to criticize a sick man for staying in bed.

10. *Absenteeism is on the upswing,* and has been so for the past three decades even though the general health of the nation has improved. Insecurity is no longer the force it once was in getting people to work. They do not fear job loss. Moreover, affluence has created a greater demand for leisure, and sometimes employees take a day or so off to pursue some private venture regardless of what it does to the company's attendance record.

Of course, these statements about absenteeism are generalisms and should be considered as such. Every company should analyze its absenteeism problem according to its own special situation. Every manager should consider each case of excessive absenteeism individually and use those corrective measures that are most likely to win a positive response from the employee concerned. However, when management has cleared its mind of the many fallacies about absenteeism, it should be more capable of dealing with the matter realistically.

No Easy Answer to Absenteeism Control

There are two basic facts about absentee control that any experienced manager has probably discovered:

1. Regardless of the nature of a person's work, the relationship he has with his boss, his treatment, and his interest in what he is doing will be reflected in his attendance record.
2. Absenteeism is influenced by the leadership of the group's manager, the attitudes of the employees in the group, the feeling of accomplishment and recognition each individual gets from doing his particular job, and the status of the job to which the employee is assigned.

There are a multitude of nostrums and sure-cure remedies for absenteeism that many executives unthinkingly accept and on which they occasionally act. Chances are, they are no more effective than a poster urging employees to "Keep Costs Down" is helpful in combating waste unless it is implemented with a sound program of sustained action.

Lewis L. Newman, president of the A. L. Smith Iron Company, commented on this very point when he said: "How often have you heard that a high absenteeism rate is caused by a relatively few employees who are absenteeism-prone? We tested this theory at my company. The evidence is that when the so-called absenteeism-prone employee is removed from a certain group another takes his place. What's more, we have all seen how the fellow who frequently misses work often changes his habits for the better when his job is changed or his assignment becomes more interesting. Another doubtful method of cutting down absenteeism is to ask the often-absent employee, 'Why?' His explanation will probably be confused. You wouldn't expect him to say, 'I stayed home because my work bores me silly,' or, 'I wasn't here because I can't stand my boss.' "

Mr. Newman's observations, although controversial (especially regarding his point on the interview after the absence), at least provoke thought in that he suggests management should follow a "buyer beware" policy in the treatment of absenteeism so far as its own organization is concerned. Generally, if an employee knows full well that when he returns to work after a day or two at home his boss will talk to him to find out what was wrong, he will not take a day off just because he feels like it. But it is also true that most employees have good attendance records anyhow; so, once again, the average manager finds that he is concentrating on a few absenteeism-prone people in such discussions.

A Penalty May Be the Only Answer

It is fashionable today for many persons to deplore the punitive approach in the maintenance of any kind of discipline. Certainly it should be used only as a last resort. But the knowledge that such a weapon is available and will be used if all else fails is undoubtedly the only reason why some people observe rules and regulations. If the fear of retribution were totally removed in the enforcement of law and order, the misfits, the socially maladjusted, and the criminal element would have a field day. Yet the doctrine of permissiveness is increasingly promulgated, even though all anyone has to do is to look at the afternoon paper to be convinced of its failure.

The children's program "Captain Kangaroo" reflected this trend in its version of the story of Little Red Riding

Hood and the wolf. Adults will recall that, when Little Red Riding Hood visited her grandmother to bring a gift of food, a wolf she had met on the way had gotten there first and had eaten the little old lady in one fast mouthful. When Riding Hood entered the cottage, she made a few brief observations on the changed appearance of her grandmother and received some decidedly unsatisfactory answers. Then the wolf leaped out of bed and would have devoured Little Red Riding Hood but for the timely appearance of a woodsman who dispatched the wolf with his handy ax. The grandmother was miraculously restored to life (in some versions), and everybody lived happily ever afterward.

This is not the way they tell it today. The wolf visits the grandmother, all right, but he only locks the old lady in the closet. When Riding Hood arrives and gets around to the comment, "What long teeth you have!" the wolf jumps out of bed and snaps, "The better to eat your cookies with, my dear!" He has every intention of locking Riding Hood in the closet with the grandmother, but the brave woodsman arrives in the nick of time and gives the wolf a lecture on his socially unacceptable behavior. The wolf, thoroughly chastened, apologizes to all concerned and, promising to lead a better life, returns to the forest.

Anybody who believes such drivel—even the tiny tots for whom it is intended—will be a setup for the first mugger he is unfortunate enough to meet. But it is non-violent and there is no retribution for outrageous behavior, only sympathy and understanding. So it serves its purpose of being a fairy tale. Even a youngster growing up in these times knows better, though. Life is simply not that way at all.

It's Up to the Supervisor

To straighten out any operational problem—and this includes breakdowns in any area of discipline—a supervisor must follow a three-step approach: (1) Assemble the facts, (2) analyze the facts, and (3) reach a reasonable conclusion on what to do that is based on those facts.

If it is evident that an absenteeism problem is developing in a department, it is the responsibility of the supervisor in charge to take quick remedial action. The control of absenteeism is almost totally in the hands of those supervisors and department heads who are immediately concerned with the direction of employees.

Each supervisor should have an understanding as to why management considers absenteeism a problem of major significance. Dollars and cents alone is a powerful argument. The absenteeism rate for industry generally is 3 percent per year (according to most estimates), and it does not take a financial expert to see that this constitutes a major business expense.

Mr. Newman, in pointing out the price industry pays for absenteeism, cites these items:

1. Disrupted schedules, production slowdowns, and customer inconvenience.
2. Idle machinery and unused investment due to absent employees.
3. Higher training costs.
4. Waste and inefficiency because substitutes are working on assignments for which they are untrained or for which they are out of practice.
5. Overtime pay.

6. Additional employees on the payroll to take the place of absent persons. (Mr. Newman claims some companies staff as high as 5 percent above their actual needs to be prepared for predictable absence.)

The most effective way to keep absences down is to develop an effective system of controls and to maintain constant vigilance. Any relaxation of effort or slackness in managerial consistency in the enforcement of its rules, including attendance, may have unfortunate consequences. The following recommendations may be helpful in establishing a good system of absenteeism controls and administering attendance policies fairly and firmly.

1. *Train supervisors to carry out their responsibilities for absenteeism control.* High attendance is generally a sign of high morale. If a supervisor cannot rely on the presence of his full workforce, he will be forced to improvise to handle his assignment, and his effectiveness will suffer. He should make it a point to talk to any subordinate returning to work after an absence (whatever the reason), if only to make sure of the employee's state of health. When an employee is ill, his superior should keep in touch with him during his sickness and visit him if possible. When he reports back to work, the employee should be welcomed and made to feel that he was missed.

2. *Insist that supervisors maintain good records.* Accurate weekly and monthly absence reports are necessary instruments of control. They warn the manager of possible trouble spots and enable him to forestall serious difficulties by prompt remedial action.

3. *Instruct supervisors how to make use of report data.* Statistics intelligently analyzed can help a manager identify the cause of a problem. Absence reports tell a supervisor

how the absence rate of his group compares with those of other groups. Indicating absences by job classification, sex, and age, they also enable a manager to pinpoint exactly which employees are pushing his absenteeism record into the "excessive" category.

4. *Train supervisors in the value of consistency.* A crash program of stiff penalties may clear up an absentee problem, but only on a short-term basis. An alert manager uses more constructive methods and seldom needs to resort to harsh measures. Supervisors and executives who have earned the respect and confidence of their subordinates usually are not plagued by an absenteeism problem. They have built team spirit and cooperative attitudes into their training methods. Each employee knows his job is important and his presence essential to the efficiency of the unit. He is *motivated* to come to work, not compelled to do so.

5. *Stress leadership in supervisory training.* High morale is the product of good leadership, and absenteeism is a rarity in a group that is motivated positively. An employee who knows that his absence has hurt the effort of his organization, and that he has failed both his fellow employees and his boss by missing work, strives to keep an absence-free attendance record. On the other hand, an excessive rate of absenteeism generally is a symptom of serious deficiencies in management leadership. Employees are dissatisfied with their working conditions, their jobs, and their treatment, and this is reflected in their attitudes and possibly in their attendance record. The manager who has problems in any of these aspects of employee relations will not cure absenteeism (except temporarily) by harsh discipline. In such a situation, chances are that another manager is needed to put things straight.

2

The Late-Arriving Employee

Tardiness and absenteeism are similar problems. The absent employee does not get to work at all, while the late-arriving employee only half gets there. Both are costly to a company in that they impair its efficiency, and both are signs of disciplinary difficulties. However, excessive absenteeism may stem from many causes, such as job dissatisfaction, lack of motivation, poor working conditions, or lack of managerial leadership; while tardiness, if widespread, is usually a sign of supervisory laxness or indifference. "If the boss doesn't care when I'm five minutes late," reasons the employee, "there is no need to hurry. Besides, what difference does it make?"

When there is no penalty, such as "docking," for tardiness, a supervisor who does not insist on punctuality may soon find that he has few starters when the working day begins. Employees straggle in anywhere from five to fifteen minutes late and would be surprised if there was any comment about their laggard arrival. The fact that they are late does not necessarily mean that they are dissatisfied with their jobs or even with their leadership. It is simply an indication that punctuality has not been emphasized as a principle of good management.

In plant or hourly operations, employees may be required to punch a time clock, and if they register late they suffer a financial penalty. For purposes of imposing the wage deduction, the hour may be divided into fifteen-minute segments, and if an employee is three minutes late he cannot begin work until fifteen minutes after the hour. Therefore, the very system assures that a tardy employee will lose a quarter of an hour of working time, regardless of whether he is late by one minute or ten, and this in itself is somewhat wasteful. But then time clocks are mechanical, and to attempt to calculate deductions on a to-the-minute basis would be difficult. It might also be mentioned that more and more companies are abandoning time clocks in favor of a more positive means of checking attendance and punctuality.

The Three Kinds of Tardiness

Behavioral scientists who have studied the problem of lateness give certain reasons for it which may be useful to management in formulating rules governing punctuality and to supervisors and managers who must deal with late-arriving employees. They say—and this is a general statement—that there are three basic kinds of tardiness. They are:

1. *No one's fault—that is, accidental.* The train or bus was late; bad weather slowed down traffic; there was a car mishap along the way.
2. *The fault of the employee.* Fatigue due to moonlighting or too much overtime; overindulgence; lack of motivation; emotional problems.
3. *The fault of the supervisor.* Management indifference; laxness in the enforcement of disciplinary rules; failure to give positive leadership.

It is obvious that the first reason for lateness causes no real difficulty for a manager, but the other two are significant. If lack of punctuality is the employee's own fault, it is a sign that group discipline is below standard, and this may well be attributable to a failure of leadership. If the supervisor is at fault, that is clear evidence that he has neglected to discipline himself.

The Department of Labor provides some interesting facts about lateness that perhaps puncture certain beliefs some supervisors and executives appear to hold. The Department says that older employees usually have better punctuality records than their younger colleagues; that there is no relationship between the distance an employee travels to and from work and his punctuality performance; and that unhappy or discontented employees are quite likely to have poor attendance and punctuality reports. It also adds the not-unexpected fact that the day after a holiday is also a time when the index on tardiness is likely to show a high reading.

Other facts about tardiness: (1) Poor employee performance so far as punctuality is concerned is likely to stem from some situation or condition within the company and has little to do with any outside factor that may affect the employee. (2) The type of relationship established between superior and subordinate may be reflected in the latter's attendance and punctuality record. (3) Usually, habitual latecomers are only a small minority in any given group, but statistically they account for a department's excessive absenteeism and tardiness. (4) Female employees are more likely to be late than men because they more frequently have pressing family matters to which they must attend or minor sicknesses which incapacitate them briefly.

The Role of the Supervisor

Since tardiness is costly in terms of money and lost efficiency, and since it is a problem that can be controlled only by front-line management, it is apparent that the only intelligent course a company can take is to train its supervisors and department heads in stressing the importance of punctuality and, on the negative side, to enforce rules dealing with lateness fairly, consistently, and with the flexibility of good judgment. If an employee does not like his work or his boss, he finds little difficulty in persuading himself that some private matter takes precedence over it, and when he does go jobward he moves like Shakespeare's schoolboy, on laggard feet, so that it is no wonder he does not always arrive on time. Therefore, the ability of the individual manager as a leader and as a motivator will determine the effectiveness of a company in the administration of this aspect of its discipline program.

Any management that wishes to inculcate the habit of promptness in its employees should begin with the supervisors and line managers. They have the "make or break" power over the success of the company's effort; and, unless they assume the responsibilities of affirmative leadership in the full meaning of that term, no program will achieve results. As Napoleon observed, the morale and discipline of an army are no better than those of the junior officers who are visible to the men. This reflection certainly holds true, as well, for an organization operating in a society that emphasizes individual freedom and must rely chiefly on such positive methods as persuasion, incentives, and leadership to gain its objectives.

What, then, should a supervisor be trained to do in order to reduce tardiness to a minimal problem? Here are some suggestions that reflect the practices of many major companies which have cut the problem of lateness down to easily handled dimensions.

1. *Administer rules firmly and consistently, but with*

flexibility. The late-arriving employee should not be allowed to think he has gotten away with his failure to report on time. However, it would be foolish to crack down so hard on lateness that an employee prefers to stay home with the excuse of sickness than brave his boss's lectures. Such an attitude only compounds a case of tardiness into an absentee problem. Rather, the manager should endeavor to find out why the employee is late and point out to him the effect that his lack of promptness has had on the working efficiency of his group.

2. *Identify and observe habitual offenders strictly.* Accurate day-by-day records provide the supervisor with information on an employee's attendance and punctuality performance. Each supervisor should strive to discover the cause of an employee's lateness (it may be some temporary personal problem) and treat each case on its own merits. However, an employee should be left in no doubt that it is up to him to correct his dilatory habits, and it is usually a good idea to ask him how he plans to do so. If persuasion and counsel finally fail, discipline must be applied and penalties imposed—even to dismissal.

3. *Give recognition to good attendance and punctuality records.* The very fact that the boss has noticed an employee's conscientious attendance and punctuality record and appreciates it is encouraging not only to the person concerned but to his associates.

4. *Make certain that employees understand the rules governing punctuality.* Some companies distribute copies of attendance and punctuality regulations and make sure that their supervisors discuss these rules with employees. It is the fault of management's laxness and failure to communicate if an employee can plead, "I didn't know the rule," when charged with an offense.

5. *Be sure other employees know about special conditions that have caused management to relax its rules on punctuality in the case of a particular employee.* If an employee is forced to report to work late for private reasons and has his boss's permission to do so, other employees should be advised that in this case special circumstances made such a decision fair and advisable. Otherwise, the supervisor may be unfairly suspected of playing favorites.

6. *Strive for participation.* Use training to inculcate in each employee a sense of belonging to the group. Try to make him feel that his work is important, his ideas and suggestions are needed, and his contribution to the overall effort is valuable. When employees believe they are essential to the success of an organization, they are punctual.

7. *Establish a good example.* The supervisor sets the pace. His attitude and example provide a guide for subordinates, and their actions and attitudes are a reflection of his own. If the supervisor is late himself, the chances are that the employees will not be prompt. If the supervisor is indifferent about punctuality in the employees, they too will regard it lightly.

3

Labor Turnover: Is It All Bad?

No workforce remains static. New people are always coming in to fill the manpower needs of the organization, and people are always leaving. As an enterprise grows, it requires additional employees. When veterans quit, retire, or are terminated, they must be replaced. Since World War II there has been a seller's market, so far as job seekers are concerned, and employment opportunities are abundant—especially for men and women who have skills, talents, or abilities that industry requires. Therefore, the person who is dissatisfied with his present position (whatever the reason), or who finds what he considers a better opportunity elsewhere, is likely to become a statistic in the firm's labor turnover report.

Once again, from the standpoint of positive discipline, the turnover problem—so far as morale, job satisfaction, and competitive group effort are concerned—is largely in the hands of line management. To be sure, an enlightened company will provide intelligent policy on wages and fringe benefits, working conditions, and employment security. Such a firm will also conduct a sound recruitment and selection program. But, after the applicant has been hired, the administration of policy and his relationship with the company will be based on the rapport that exists between him and his superior. If they fulfill their responsibilities and if other conditions are satisfactory, turnover will be reasonable and attributable to factors other than poor morale or employee discontent.

A degree of labor turnover is healthy for a company. A management that emphasizes job security and relies on the same people year after year is likely to lose its competitive thrust. Executives and supervisors grow old and tired on their jobs; they lose their drive, and so fresh ideas are not forthcoming. New blood is always essential to continued progress.

An executive of a major tool company commented on this when he said, "We had too many people in responsible positions who had grown soft in their positions. A drastic shake-up in management was the only answer. We were forced to give some of our department heads, even some of our top executives who had reached 45 or 50 and were doing nothing, the opportunity for a second career elsewhere. It was hard medicine, but it worked."

A Yardstick for Labor Turnover

Labor statisticians measure personnel turnover by expressing the percentage of average workforce over a period of time that is represented by new people. But as Carl Heyel says in *The Supervisor's Basic Management Guide,* published by McGraw-Hill in 1965, "It can be seen that if the labor force remains constant over a period, you would get the same percentage by dividing the number who are hired by the average workforce, since those who leave are exactly matched by those who are hired. However, if the average workforce changes the arithmetic isn't that simple. In that case, the measure is accepted to be the percentage obtained by dividing the accessions or withdrawals, whichever is smaller, by the average workforce. A labor turnover figure expressed on a monthly basis would be multiplied by 12 to get the turnover on a yearly basis. Thus a company or a department which has a turnover of 2 percent per month has a 24 percent turnover per year." And, as Mr. Heyel observes, it is not unusual to find turnover rates of 25 to 50 percent per year in manufacturing companies.

Statistics on labor turnover have no direct relationship to the problem of discipline. If the coming and going of a firm's employees is natural, and if it maintains its competitive position, labor turnover may indeed be a sign of progress.

It is only when employees leave their jobs in large numbers because they are dissatisfied with working conditions, the policies of management, the competence of their supervisors, their pay, or their opportunity for advancement that turnover becomes evidence of internal disciplinary problems within a company. For example, the young executive who leaves his company because another has offered him income and authority far beyond what he now enjoys cannot be compared to the man who retreats to employment elsewhere because he thinks his present firm is headed for financial disaster and does not want to be on board when the ship goes down.

Why Do Employees Quit?

Therefore, before a management concerns itself too much about labor turnover as related to positive discipline, it should carefully review the reasons why employees are leaving and why it is difficult to attract adequate replacements. If labor turnover is excessive, the first step toward getting to the root cause of the problem is to analyze the cause of "quits." Certainly, if valued employees are departing, something is very wrong.

Managements that have been confronted with high labor turnover because positive discipline and employee morale are below standard claim that the reasons usually lie in poor supervisory or executive leadership. They list the following causes of negative labor turnover, all traceable to poor management.

1. *Overloading of a subordinate.* An almost certain way for a manager to force a key man into resigning is to burden him with too much work and, because he is

valuable where he is, to deny him opportunity for advancement. Such a person becomes discontented and frustrated if his efforts and abilities go unrewarded and unrecognized. No ambitious employee will be satisfied with his boss's private esteem if he thinks his career is blocked because of the latter's selfishness. The only cure for such a problem is intelligent leadership, recognition of superior performance, and promotion for the deserving.

2. *Lack of opportunity.* Even if a supervisor or executive is doing a fine job in handling his people, he cannot keep the ambitious employee satisfied forever if there are no opportunities for advancement. This may not be the manager's fault. There may simply be no openings above to which capable people can be promoted. However, a wise leader will make certain that his subordinates know their promotion chances at the time of hire; he will not hold out false hopes. He also realizes that many young people want to move too fast too quickly and that their estimate of their abilities occasionally exceeds their actual worth. So he gives them special counsel and trains them to be ready for more responsible assignments when they come. Of course, no boss can keep all his good men. But the executive or supervisor who knows how to develop people will provide his company with capable managers for the future and increase his value to the company by doing so.

3. *Lack of communication.* The employee who cannot make his complaints known and believes his boss does not give him the consideration to which he is entitled is likely to become dissatisfied and unhappy. Subordinates want a superior to be accessible; they expect him to listen to them and understand their problems. The manager who has the skilled human relations touch can smooth out the

wrinkles in employee relations and thus maintain high morale.

4. *Inadequate compensation.* The employee who believes that he is being shortchanged in his paycheck, whether or not his belief is valid, is usually in the market for a job somewhere else. Compensation inequities are a major cause of both labor turnover and grievances. An experienced manager makes certain that each subordinate receives a careful explanation of how the pay for his job is calculated during his orientation training—an explanation that includes the value of his job in relation to other jobs. When an employee has a justifiable complaint about his wages or salary, a good manager will inform the executives responsible for wage and salary administration and try to get the proper adjustment made, even if this means going to his own superior.

5. *Poor placement.* The employee who is badly placed in his assignment is worried and afraid of his job. If he lacks the ability to perform properly and knows deep down that he is in over his head, he will probably give notice. It is easier to do that than to admit the job is too much for him. Similarly, the person who is given an assignment that totally lacks challenge will soon become bored and frustrated. Proper job placement is essential if a company wishes to retain its good people.

6. *Generally incompetent management.* Capable subordinates simply refuse to work for an incompetent manager—that is, for very long. Arbitrary, indifferent, and vacillating supervision is a prime cause of high labor turnover. But the manager who carries out his training and communication responsibilities effectively, who is perceptive and understanding of employee feelings and knows each person as an individual, who makes his people

feel that they belong to a successful organization and that he recognizes and appreciates their contribution to the effort of the group, is not bothered by labor turnover. Such a boss attracts capable men and women. They want to be on his team.

Guides to the Containment of Negative Labor Turnover

The manager who wants to be successful in his job of controlling negative labor turnover may find the following suggestions worth considering.

1. *Supervisors and executives must administer rules and policy equitably, impartially, and consistently.* Employees should always feel that they are being treated fairly and can get a hearing from the boss.

2. *Communication must be effective.* Employees must be kept informed on how they are doing in their jobs. When a person is deficient in some area of his performance, he must have a clear understanding of exactly why and how he is not meeting standards. Then he must be given the training or coaching he needs to improve.

3. *Supervisors and executives must be available and receptive to the ideas of subordinates.* Recognition and credit must be given to persons who perform outstandingly. The manager who is too busy to listen to employee problems, who shows no interest in their progress, and who brushes off their questions can drive away more good people than the best recruitment program can ever secure.

4. *Training must be thorough.* Employees must be given the coaching and training they require to perform

at top capacity. The manager who neglects this important duty is failing in his role of leadership.

5. *New policies, methods, and procedures must be explained.* Careful explanations as to why a company has adopted new policies, methods, and procedures and how employees will be affected as individuals by such changes provide the key to understanding and cooperation. If a manager or a company gets the reputation of being arbitrary or dictatorial, labor turnover will climb.

6. *Judgment must be used in placement.* Managers must have an accurate knowledge of the skills, talents, and abilities of subordinates, and place them in assignments which interest and challenge them. Promotions should be carefully made, and merit should be the overriding factor in choosing who is to be advanced. If a manager is thought by employees to be 'playing favorites' in assigning work or in making promotions, employees lose confidence in him, morale drops, and there is excessive turnover among capable people.

7. *Leadership must be strong.* Firm, consistent, fair leadership is the foundation of high morale. Employee morale is in itself a company's best protection against negative labor turnover.

6

OUR
CARELESS CULTURE

Waste—Byproduct of a Civilization
of Abundance

WASTE IS APPARENTLY A SYMPTOM of an affluent society.
Maxims such as "A penny saved is a penny earned" and
"Keep a dollar today, and tomorrow your dollars will keep
you" do not have much appeal nowadays. The buying
power of money has been so eroded by inflation that a
person hardly bothers to pick up a dropped penny, and
high taxes make it almost impossible for the average man
or woman to build up a retirement income out of his own
resources. Instead, people depend on government- and
company-financed pension programs; dread of that "rainy
day" does not seem to affect the attitude or habits of the
public.

Waste is an indication of lack of personal self-discipline;

for, as has often been observed, waste control is essentially a state of mind. Some years ago a major railroad company estimated that its annual bill for pencils, paper clips, and typing paper ran into thousands of dollars annually, and one of its executives observed that this outlay could probably be reduced by more than 50 percent if employees would be more careful with company supplies. And practically everybody has heard the old story attributed to the president of a spice company. "The amount of mustard a customer leaves on the stick or in the jar is the measure of our profit," he is supposed to have said. "The customer has the right to waste our product. He pays for it. We don't! It's our job to get the mustard into the jar with as little loss as possible."

The Problem of Waste Control

Perhaps the most severe challenge to management at the present time is summed up in one big question: "How does a company keep its costs in line with the customer's ability to pay, maintain the quality of its products or services, and still make a profit?"

The answer may be divided into two parts: (1) Increase productivity or efficiency. (2) Keep a sharp eye on unnecessary costs. The first may be done by better machines, better equipment, better methods. The second can be accomplished by alert management leadership which instills in each employee the belief that, when he fights waste and takes a personal responsibility for keeping costs down, he is in reality protecting his own job security and assuring his future.

To build such an employee attitude is probably the hardest task a manager has. After all, the example of leadership in this nation is not one that inspires thrift. Taxes—municipal, state, and federal—bite deeply into everyone's income, and the government outlay of the funds it collects is hardly calculated to convince the average citizen that his money is always being wisely spent. Therefore, it is only human nature for a person to reason, "Why be a patsy? I might as well get my share. There is no need to bother about company supplies, scrap, idle time, or fudged expense accounts. It's management's money, and the company can write off the cost of any loss on its income-tax return."

Such an attitude on the part of many employees and even some managers is certainly a factor in rising business costs, and it is clear evidence of a lack of positive organizational discipline. All one has to do is to read the account of the difficulties business is having in coping with the petty dishonesty of employees, let alone waste control, to understand the depth and ramifications of the problem. Waste is dry rot in the foundation of accomplishment, and the instant an executive relaxes in his vigilant effort to keep costs down and efficiency of operations up, it sets in. How far it will extend necessarily depends on management's success in creating the right climate of personnel relations. The day-to-day training supervisors and managers give subordinates will determine in large measure whether each one understands that high cost is his personal enemy and knows how important it is to take care of his company's tools, equipment, and machinery and be economical in his use of supplies.

125

Leadership and Waste Control

The manager who has established the best record in cost reduction and waste control has certain distinguishing characteristics that mark his leadership.

1. *He has the true management attitude.* He plans, organizes, and directs efficiently. His instructions are precise and logical.

2. *His standards are high*—the standards he sets for himself, and the standards he requires subordinates to meet. Subordinates know exactly what is expected of them and whether or not they are measuring up in their performance.

3. *His training is effective and systematic.* He leaves nothing to chance. When new methods or procedures are introduced, they are accompanied by a careful explanation as to why they are superior to the old way from the standpoint of efficiency and costs. Training is never neglected. When employees are given different jobs, or when changes are made in old ones, proper instruction is provided to make sure that employee mistakes and loss of time because of uncertainty or indifference are kept to a minimum.

4. *He fulfills his full responsibility in employee selection.* The new employee is a big investment for a company, and the experienced manager does his best to choose wisely. In a subordinate's early training this kind of manager is thorough and watchful. He strives to give everyone in his group the instruction and coaching required to insure superior waste-proof performance as quickly as possible.

5. *His follow-up is consistent.* The effective manager is meticulous in follow-up because he understands its importance to efficient control. However, he is discreet and

tactful in his methods. As long as a subordinate is performing satisfactorily, he may not even be aware that his superior has such detailed knowledge of his activities. But, if he lets things go and his work falls below acceptable standards, his boss will take quick action.

A spirit of positive discipline is management's best protection against high costs. Therefore, a manager's understanding of human needs and his ability to motivate people are basic to his success in cost control. The effort must be steady and constant, and training and communication are the only means by which he can obtain results. While a highly publicized program of waste reduction may produce dramatic results for the short term, if management relaxes after its completion, employees will quickly return to their old habits. Nor can a system of penalties guarantee results. It will simply convince the employee that, when he plays fast and loose with company supplies, loafs on the job, or is careless or wasteful in his working practices, his major worry is not to get caught at it. He has no sense of personal responsibility for keeping expenses down and sees no reason why he should cooperate to achieve a management objective in which he has no interest and from which he derives no benefit.

Areas Where Costs Can Soar

The modern industrial or business organization employs expert staff people—time-study men, cost accountants, cost engineers, methods analysts—whose sole responsibility it is to establish costs, find precise ways of measuring them, and supply management with information on where and how if costs exceed expected standards. But, according to studies made in the field, line managers are responsible for as much as 74 percent of operating costs (exclusive of the cost of raw materials), and the effectiveness of a company's endeavors to reduce waste will depend on how well they do their job. A supervisor undoubtedly has at least a degree of control over how much money his management spends on the following items.

1. *Direct labor.* Poorly trained, indifferent employees are inefficient and expensive, no matter how little or how much they are paid. Employees or machines that are idle because a manager failed to plan properly cut deeply into a company's profits and its competitiveness.

2. *Scrap and spoilage.* High scrap and spoilage records are an indication of poor employee selection, inadequate training, and lack of individual motivation. A manager who tolerates below-standard performance cannot expect subordinates to concern themselves with cost reduction.

3. *Supplies.* Loose controls and carelessness in the handling of supplies or equipment contribute to a dollar drain no healthy management can afford. This is a problem over which line managers exercise great influence, and their ability to build into employee practices concern over the irresponsible use of company supplies or equipment determines, to a great degree, their effectiveness as supervisors or executives.

4. *Indirect labor.* The line manager may not have too much control over indirect labor costs, but his ability to plan and organize the work of his group certainly affects it. The price of indirect as compared to direct labor is frequently too high because of undue handling charges.

5. *Breakage.* Machine breakdowns and tools long overdue for repair can be costly items in a company budget. Some of this expense can be reduced by line managers who

are alert in inspection and who know the value of preventive maintenance. Well-trained, efficient employees
are themselves a protection against excessive maintenance
costs, and their training is the direct responsibility of the
manager.

6. *Overtime.* Extra work at premium pay is sometimes
necessary, but it is the most expensive way of getting the
job done. Prolonged overtime leads to increased absences,
habitual lateness, higher accident rates, and a decline in
productivity. If overtime is needed because of inadequate
planning, organizing, or scheduling on the part of a
manager, he should carefully restudy his methods and take
prompt corrective measures.

Motivation Is Essential

Personal motivation is the only lasting answer to management's war against waste. It is just another aspect of
positive group discipline.

The fact that major industries today are large and employ many thousands of people does not mean that
management must sacrifice the personal touch. To get
around the problems of the gigantic, impersonal enterprise,
many companies have broken their operations down into
small, easily managed units and scattered them throughout
the country. There is no doubt that people who are members of a huge organization often do not feel a close and
intimate relationship with it and may not identify themselves with its interests unless a special effort is made to
motivate them effectively.

Even labor unions are encountering this difficulty.
Rank-and-file members, many top union executives com-

plain, no longer feel close to their organization. Frequently they do not even agree with the objectives of their leaders, much less support them. An unidentified Steelworker officer has been quoted in a national newspaper in these terms: "Union members today don't attend meetings, take little interest in union activities, and, outside of their interest in how much we can get for them, are indifferent to what we are doing."

A Plan for Waste Control

The fact that the problem is complex and difficult does not mean that it cannot be solved by intelligent management action. The Monsanto Chemical Company attributes the stability and high productivity of one of its assembly-line operations to its positive motivational techniques. The assembly line is staffed entirely by women, and the company says that, since its program was introduced, labor turnover has dropped 12 percent, productivity has increased as much as 20 percent, rejects have dropped about 30 percent, and absenteeism has declined to 3 percent as compared to the industrial average for women of 5 percent.

Here are some of the features of the plan:

1. Thorough pre-employment training of workers, with hiring dependent on testing.
2. Uniform hourly rates with five- to six-cent increases every three months plus a yearly review.
3. Job rotation to give each operator a chance at every job on the line.
4. Management-employee trouble-shooting meetings at

which joint solutions to mutual problems are reached.

5. No time clocks—employees keep their own time records.
6. Name tags worn by all employees.
7. Common lunchroom facilities for all employees, including top executives.
8. Work cubicles with individual name plates.

Rial Simmons, personnel superintendent, makes these comments: "Employees are best motivated through self-fulfillment. Training, job rotation, and employee participation in decision making are the key ingredients to the success of our approach."

Such a plan may not be adaptable to all operations, or useful to every company, but the principles on which it is based can certainly be applied elsewhere. It does little good to rely on preachments and arguments, no matter how solidly they are based on fact. A person can have at best only an academic interest in anything in which he feels no personal involvement—that is, so long as he retains even a degree of freedom in deciding for himself whether or not the goal is worth his effort. There are many methods by which a leader can persuade subordinates to do as he wishes, and it is quite true that in a totalitarian state fear can produce astonishing effects. The galley slave, for example, kept rowing because he had no other choice and wished to avoid the lash. But in a free society leaders must rely on more positive motivators such as pride, recognition, self-interest, ambition, and individual involvement, and this holds true in waste reduction as it does in every other area of positive discipline.

The Problem in Perspective

Commenting on the tremendous importance of loss prevention and the essentiality of its control to a manager, Dr. Ronald C. Horn, of the University of South Carolina, observed, "To replace a $100 loss with a $100 profit, an office supply retailer must sell 4,750,000 paper clips, a publisher must sell 17,500 newspapers, a department store must sell 8,000 pairs of socks, a supermarket must ring up 357 $20 sales, 15 television sets must be built, and a property and liability insurer must collect 3,226 premium dollars."

These figures put the problem into perspective. Clearly, any management that is lax in its efforts to combat waste is likely to end up in the graveyard of bankruptcy, with the notice on its tombstone "Here Lies a Company That Cost Too Much."

While the contemporary climate of society is not one to encourage habits of economy in people, the fact that the fight against the high cost of waste, inefficiency, and complacency is an uphill struggle does not make it less necessary. Success in such an effort requires a constant and determined attack on cost-causing waste in every area of operations; and, although the individual manager may win no dramatic victories along the way, his consistent effort will produce visible results in his company's profit and loss statement and in employee attitudes. The experienced manager has found that the drive against waste is never over, that no triumph is final. It is a fight that must be won every day and must be conducted systematically and thoroughly.

The following suggestions may be helpful in inculcating waste-control attitudes and habits in employee practices and points of view.

1. *Plan carefully.* Identify the causes of waste—inadequate training, indifferent employee attitudes, incorrect use of machinery or equipment, poor scheduling or work assignments—and eliminate them.

2. *Organize effectively.* Employee participation is the key to cooperation, and cost control is a matter of teamwork. A manager must have the support of his subordinates to reduce excessive waste. Employee ideas and recommendations should be encouraged and accepted when they have merit.

3. *Train carefully.* Well-trained employees work efficiently, and waste control is an automatic part of their working methods.

4. *Specify objectives.* Successful waste-control programs cannot be conducted in a vacuum. Employees must have an accurate understanding of what they are expected to accomplish and must be kept informed as to the progress they are making toward their goal. Recognition and appreciation of accomplishment instill group pride.

5. *Establish high standards.* The very fact that an employee has the ability to meet the standards of excellence required by a successful manager sets him apart from the mediocre worker and increases his self-respect and pride in individual and team accomplishment. Good performance standards that are understood and accepted by employees are insurance against waste-producing attitudes.

6. *Neglect no details.* The whole of any problem is comprised of its small parts. This is particularly true in waste reduction. An alert manager is aware of the inherent possibility of waste in every phase of his operation; he does not ignore careless practices because each one in itself is

not too expensive, nor does he rely on expensive improvisation to complete an assignment because he failed to plan properly in advance.

7. *Study new methods.* New methods that are more efficient and less expensive in terms of time, money, and employee effort are tools with a keen cutting edge against high costs. A major responsibility of every manager, no matter at what level, is to study and review his methods of operation constantly and to seek better and faster ways of getting results.

8. *Keep good records.* Records are invaluable in recognizing causes of waste and pinpointing excessive costs. Until causes have been precisely identified, no constructive program can be developed to eliminate them.

9. *Communicate intelligently.* Good communication sustains interest and can be used to make waste reduction personally meaningful to employees.

10. *Insist on order.* Good housekeeping is a symbol of a manager's attitude toward cost control. Waste flourishes in an environment where slovenliness prevails.

Who Takes What from Whom?

Another problem that is closely associated with waste reduction and cost control is the difficulty many managements are facing as they try to enforce standards of simple honesty among employees. The annual bill that industry pays for petty thievery is staggering; some estimate it as more than a billion dollars a year.

The worst of it is that many an employee who takes a ream of typewriting paper home for his personal use or "borrows" some tools from the company storeroom which he does not expect to return hardly considers his act dishonest at all. "The boss won't miss the paper," or, "Maybe I'll return the tools some day," he reasons. And then, to further justify his behavior, he rationalizes, "Besides, other people are doing the same thing."

The simple fact that they work in a company is to some employees ample excuse for helping themselves to whatever they need that is unwatched and available. Not only are they not ashamed of their deeds; they may even take a perverse pride in their larceny. A maintenance employee at a lumber company built a garage from material he had filched from his unsuspecting boss and was surprised and angry when the company finally trapped him in the act of stealing and dismissed him from his job, even though there was no legal prosecution. A mechanic proudly displayed his cellar tool shop to friends and neighbors and bragged that his employer had unknowingly provided him with the equipment needed for his hobby. Indeed, if he had not talked so much his company might never have learned of his activities and terminated him. These are typical examples of the kind of employee dishonesty that is becoming increasingly prevalent today.

When well-meaning people argue that if society could cure its social ills it would simultaneously cure its difficulties with crime and related evils, they have only to look at who is doing the pilfering in department stores and supermarkets. All too frequently the perpetrators are men or women who certainly do not need to steal in order to eat or to support a family. Nor do the dishonest employees of industry and business fit neatly into the category of the disadvantaged. Rather, the record shows that it is theft by the so-called respectable citizens, employees and managers who hold positions of some trust in their companies, that is at an all-time high. Yet social condemnation for their acts is hardly evident except, perhaps, when they are so unfortunate as to be caught.

A supervisor in a manufacturing plant described the situation in these words: "It's easy for employees to get in the habit of what they call 'borrowing.' But borrowing with no intention of paying back, or without even the lender's knowing about it, is putting 'sugar coating' around the unpleasant word 'stealing.' "

Mine and Thine

The fundamental cause of theft in industry usually boils down to slack management and loose controls, in themselves evidence of a breakdown in discipline. If an employer merely writes off his pilferage losses as necessary business expenses; if, even when a person is caught "with the goods," he restricts punishment to a token penalty or a reprimand, even the offender may become convinced that management really does not care too much and that "borrowing," provided he does not get found out, is a perquisite of his job. So he has no more feeling of repentance than does the child whose mother catches him with his fingers in the cookie jar.

Many managers say that the problem is a product of the times and that not much can be done about it. And, if there is no moral censure from either management or fellow employees when a person has the hard luck to be caught in the act of stealing, it is not surprising that people develop attitudes that are more usually attributed to Light-Fingered Harry, the scourge of the pickpocket squad, or to the Artful Dodger, the nemesis of Oliver Twist. But, since the vast majority of people would prefer to be honest and to be associated with colleagues who are honest, a harsh punitive program should not be needed to reduce pilferage to at least manageable proportions.

Many experts on the subject of employee stealing claim that a strict antitheft program may be self-defeating and that, to a certain type of person, such an approach is a challenge to his resourcefulness instead of being a deterrent. Although antithievery devices such as surprise auditing, sudden inspections, searches of employee lockers, lie-detector tests (where legal), and closed-circuit television may sometimes be necessary as a last resort against excessive thievery, their very existence indicates that employee morale is almost at the vanishing point and positive discipline no longer is possible.

An Antipilferage Checklist

Sensible management does not regard the dishonest employee lightly or treat his offense as if it did not matter. However, it places most of its dependence on more affirmative disciplinary measures, and it relies for the success of these measures on the leadership and managerial ability of individual supervisors and executives. Such a management is sufficiently realistic to develop a pattern of controls that makes thievery difficult because it is quickly and easily detected. Antitheft controls of this kind are not a cause of friction in employee relations. They generally win the cooperative support of the great majority of a company's people. A person who is himself honest is unhappy working for a company which regards him distrustfully; he does not like to be a possible suspect every time there is a case of pilferage.

The manager who would do his part in reducing his company's pilferage problem or preventing one from occurring might consider the following guidelines.

1. *Tighten up on the selection process.* Experts claim that the best place to stop the pilferer is in the employment office. Although the initial interview may be conducted by the staff people in the personnel department, a manager generally has the final say on who is hired. And, before the decision is made, there should be a thorough reference check. Prior to selection the company owes a job seeker nothing but the courtesy of a considerate and fair interview. Unless a manager is entirely satisfied with an applicant's credentials, it is simply good sense not to hire him regardless of how well qualified he may be otherwise. (This need not, of course, rule out the calculated risk of hiring an applicant, disadvantaged or not, with a criminal record—provided there is a good chance that he may make a satisfactory employee.)

2. *Keep watch on inventories.* A workable system of checks and counterchecks should be developed to control inventories. No single employee should be given the unsupervised responsibility of managing company supplies and equipment. Surprised banks and other business organizations have too often awakened one morning to find the trusted bookkeeper with 30 or more years of loyal service exposed as a crypto-expert in grand larceny. Perhaps, if the opportunity to steal had not been so wide open, he would not have succumbed to temptation. In any case, the manager who neglects his responsibility for keeping tabs on equipment, supplies, and material is asking for

problems. This is an accountability that cannot be delegated and then forgotten.

3. *Make certain company property is marked or labeled.* It is a common-sense precaution to put an ownership mark on company property. While this by itself will not put a full stop to the activities of the determined thief, at least it makes his job harder and increases the chances of detection.

4. *Keep watch on transient and spot labor.* Outsiders who have access to a plant or a place of business while they are doing a special job sometimes include dishonest persons among their number. This is especially true if the imported group of workers is large, for its size makes keeping an eye on each of its members very difficult. The alert manager knows that outside people are not governed by the rules that control regular employees, may not have been chosen by the same careful selection process, and have no loyalty to the organization. Incidentally, a cooperative employee group can be most helpful in keeping guard against pilferage from this source.

5. *Be familiar with the habits and working patterns of each employee.* Changes in an employee's job habits or practices, especially if coupled with a slight rise in pilferage, may be a signal that he no longer deserves full trust. There are frequent accounts of managers who have been duped by a trusted employee who comes to work early and remains late, not because of his conscientious effort to do a good job, but to cover up his larceny.

6. *Maintain strict rules on housekeeping.* Order is a safeguard against theft. If storerooms are not maintained with each item in its proper place, it is difficult to check on disappearances. Tools, equipment, and supplies are "easy pickings" if they are housed in such a welter of confusion

that no one can tell whether an item is "gone for good" or somebody has simply failed to return it to the shelf.

7. *Create a positive working climate.* Leadership is the foundation of morale and the molder of employee attitudes. If a subordinate believes his boss really does not care whether he helps himself to company items, it is easy to understand how he can soon reason that such a practice is really not stealing. The boss must set the standards and make them high. Managerial laxness is an invitation to carelessness; and, if employees are permitted to be individually irresponsible in their treatment of company property, management can expect its pilferage costs to climb steadily upward.

8. *Apply the rules.* No union, however powerful, can force an employer to retain a dishonest employee on its payroll—if, that is, procedural provisions of the contract are followed, the employee is proved guilty, and the penalty is in proportion to the gravity of the offense. Experts who have studied the problem of pilferage maintain that tolerant management is an encouragement to larceny. When an employee takes valuable property, he should be terminated, as should the repeat offender, even if what he takes is not too costly. Department stores and merchants with a reputation for vigorously prosecuting shoplifters and petty thieves are avoided even by so-called kleptomaniacs. Fair and reasonable rules are understood, accepted, and supported by the large majority of employees. The management that terminates a worker whose dishonesty has been established after a fair hearing need not fear any adverse reaction from his associates.

7

CHALLENGE
TO DISCIPLINE

Insubordination: Authority Under Fire

INSUBORDINATION, when equated with defiance of constituted authority, is a dangerous challenge that no organization can regard lightly or permissively if it expects to
survive. History contains account after account of such
confrontations, and strong governments have met them
with drastic counteraction. Revolution itself is nothing
more nor less than mass insubordination, and whether or
not it is justified usually has made little difference in the
fate of the power structure the rebels are trying to overturn
or modify.

Leaders who must cope with insubordination are likely
to view the reasons for it myopically and, if they have the
means and resources, to deal with it harshly. The Roman
method of meting out punishment to insubordinate troops

was short and sharp. Every tenth man in a mutinous legion, whether personally guilty or not, had his head cut off; hence the word "decimation."

The story of Captain Bligh and the good ship *Bounty* is well known to all lovers of sea stories and partons of the cinema. What middle-aged person does not remember the inimitable Charles Laughton as the harsh and arbitrary ship's captain goading First Officer Clark Gable—a debonair Mr. Christian—and the crew to such a state of fury that they finally dump Bligh and a few supporters into a small lifeboat somewhere deep in the South Pacific, then sail off to the leisurely joys of a tropical island and an idyllic life among beautiful native girls.

When Bligh and his followers finally made it back to England, the Admiralty was most unhappy. Whatever reasons the ship's company had for mutinying, their behavior could not be condoned. Justice was not the prime consideration; the effect of the men's action on naval discipline was the only worry. Regardless of what Captain Bligh had done, the mutineers had to be punished. Bligh himself finally rounded up many of them on an island retreat and brought them home to a court-martial and a hanging.

Why Employees Become Insubordinate

There are three basic reasons for insubordination.

1. The offender, perhaps to demonstrate his power, desires a deliberate confrontation with authority, and his insubordination is intended to force such a showdown. Insubordination prior to a wildcat strike may be an example of such a motive.

2. The offender, goaded beyond all endurance by what he considers the discriminatory or unfair treatment he is receiving from his superior, loses control of his temper and his judgment. Then, acting on his own initiative, with no assurance of group support, he is insubordinate. It usually happens so suddenly and spontaneously that he does not stop to consider or care about the consequences. The employee who risks his job and his future by engaging in a sudden and furious quarrel with his superior is a good illustration of this kind of insubordination.

3. Finally, there is entrapment. This occurs when a manager seeks to provoke an employee into an act of insubordination and then to penalize him for his offense. Entrapment is exemplified in the ancient "bull of the woods" supervisory maxim for getting rid of an undesirable employee: "Force the so-and-so into an argument, make him lose his temper, and then fire him for insubordination." Fortunately, the modern manager is usually too well trained to resort to such a device, and it is unlikely that he could get away with it even if he tried, particularly in a unionized company.

Degrees of Insubordination

Insubordination, whatever its cause, is a sign of breakdown in positive discipline. When it occurs, management is faced with a difficult and complex problem, and an alert company will react quickly and seek to identify the reason for it.

Almost every set of company disciplinary rules says flatly that an employee guilty of insubordination will be subject to discharge. No union would seriously challenge management's right to set up such a rule, although in practice it may well seek extenuating circumstances that will exonerate an employee charged with violating that rule.

However, the mere fact that a company is empowered to dismiss an insubordinate employee is no cure for the trouble, even if this power is unchallenged. The reason for the insubordination must be identified, and an enlightened management will strive first of all to insure full justice for the employee. Protection of a manager simply because he is a manager, despite the fact that he has acted wrongly or has made an arbitrary and unfair decision that has forced a subordinate to challenge his authority, will mean employee unrest and discontent and probably lead to future acts of insubordination.

There are types and degrees of insubordination, and an intelligent and experienced manager will deal with each one within the circumstances in which it has occurred. For example, an employee with a good record who, because of mood, state of health, or misunderstanding about an order given by his boss, has hotly refused to obey it should not be treated in the same way as the person who is a chronic rebel against management and constantly endeavors to assert his own authority in defiance of the organization. The employee who loses his head in the heat of the moment usually regrets it and hopes that future good performance will lead to the reestablishment of his past reputation. His belligerent colleague, on the other hand, will push his superior as long as he can get away with it, and unless he is brought up short his attitude will affect other employees.

A shop steward who has discovered that a particular supervisor is afraid of him and is trying to buy him off with favors will sometimes react by becoming more and more truculent. Confident that his union position will protect him from reprisal whatever he does, he has no hesitancy about being insubordinate. If he is not brought to book and made to understand that he must behave in a more responsible manner, he will usurp the authority of his boss, who eventually may lose control of his workforce.

The Rules of Discipline Applied

The wise manager works to win the support and cooperation of his group. This does not mean he is a vacillating or soft leader. The defiant subordinate who refuses to obey reasonable instructions or the equitable rules that govern employee relations cannot be tolerated and must be made to accept the need for positive discipline or dismissed from the organization to which his mere presence is a threat. An executive or a supervisor has not only the right but also the duty to compel employee compliance with fair company rules designed to maintain order.

To do so takes judgment. The employee who is charged with insubordination and penalized accordingly— so long as the charge is accurate, the hearing fair, and guilt established—has no comeback if the rule against insubordination is consistently enforced and the degree of punishment is not excessive. However, hasty, premature, or short-cut action that results in inaccurate accusations of insubordination can lead to no end of trouble—for the manager and the company.

For example, a supervisor has within his workgroup a certain employee who is a real trouble maker. But his offenses are hard to pin down. By actual deed he may not be guilty of insubordination, but he is a bad influence on other employees and is hampering the productivity and lowering the morale of the group. While this employee may never refuse to obey instructions, he is likely to go through the motions of an assignment and do just enough that management cannot claim later that he declined to do his job. He is a shop lawyer and knows how to protect himself.

In an organized company, this type of employee is usually an expert on the labor agreement. He uses the contract as a cover for his offenses and makes sure that anything he does is "protected" under its terms.

No wonder a supervisor wants to get rid of this kind of thorn-in-the-flesh employee. And the easy way? Force him into insubordination and then terminate him. The rules give the supervisor a right to dismiss an insubordinate worker. But, in actuality, the employee is guilty only of a poor attitude; he is insubordinate in his manner, true, yet he is not guilty of a specific act of insubordination at all. If the offender can prove that his boss contributed to his act of insubordination, it is the rare arbitrator who will sustain dismissal or even the imposition of a long layoff, provided the company is unwise enough to let the case get that far.

The charge of insubordination is a grave one and should never be leveled in anger. When it is made, the offense should be a demonstrable, clear-cut case of unprovoked defiance. In this event, management has no choice but to take firm remedial action. If it did otherwise, it would invite anarchy. A manager has every right to require subordinates to execute fair and reasonable orders.

In a company that has contractual relations with a

union, there is machinery which permits an employee (or the union itself) to question the acts or decisions of management that he deems unfair, arbitrary, or discriminatory. Under this procedure, if a manager cannot justify his actions, or if it is established that enforcement of the rules has been inconsistent, or if a provision of the contract has been misinterpreted, the company must reverse itself, thus guaranteeing the employee the full protection of his rights.

However, when there is disagreement between an employee and his boss, the usual practice that both unions and companies accept is to "obey now and grieve later." A person who relies so wholly on his own interpretation of the contract or has so firmly convinced himself that an order is unreasonable that he refuses on his own initiative to obey it is putting his job in jeopardy. If he is wrong, he can hardly expect to escape all penalty. There is little excuse for the man or woman who is so determined to take the law into his own hands that he ignores dispute-solving machinery established to assure justice—justice that, in reality, is the only lasting protection of his rights.

Actually, very seldom does a supervisor or an executive find that he is saddled with a chronic rebel. Even when this happens, he must remember that it is the responsibility of leadership to act coolly and objectively, especially in situations of stress and always in accordance with the rules and practices of enlightened employee relations. The boss who "blows his cool" and reacts in kind to an argumentative and trouble-making employee may be giving release to his emotions, but he is also compounding his troubles. In such a mood he cannot make certain that he is observing the rules of the union agreement and the regulations of the company or that he is exercising the reflective judgment that will produce a satisfactory answer to his difficulty. But a course of action that is grounded in common sense and is consistent with the procedures governing organizational discipline will be fair to the employee; and, whether or not it is accepted by him, it will probably be accepted and supported by everybody else. The vast majority of people who obey the rules themselves are pleased when a person who refuses to do so is put in his place.

Handling Cases of Insubordination

Single acts of insubordination are usually the problem of the line manager, who must know how to apply the rules of intelligent discipline. There are certain principles he would do well to follow when faced with a disciplinary problem that might be described as a case of insubordination. These suggestions are based on the experience of many experts in labor relations and are entirely practical. The supervisor who mentally scans this checklist before he decides whether to charge a subordinate with insubordination or with some lesser offense is in a better position to act with sound judgment.

1. *Be sure your orders are reasonable.* An employee has the right to challenge an order that he considers unreasonable. For example, instructions to an employee that he thinks might endanger his life might fall into this category. (Union contracts sometimes include this right specifically.) Of course, a subordinate seldom uses such grounds as the basis for his refusal to comply with instructions. However, before you judge that an employee's unwillingness to obey your instructions is insubordination, make certain that those instructions are entirely reason-

able and that he is qualified by experience, ability, and job classification to do any work he is being asked to perform.

2. *Be sure there has been no misunderstanding.* A manager may occasionally think an employee is being deliberately insubordinate when the truth of the matter is that much of the trouble is due to poor communication. The employee does not quite understand what is required of him and botches the assignment. The boss angrily jumps to the conclusion that this is deliberate and penalizes him for insubordination. An experienced manager makes certain that his orders are clear and accurate. If in doubt, he checks and rechecks until the subordinate fully understands what he is to do.

3. *Never accept second-hand evidence.* Insubordination is a serious charge and should never be made without a thorough investigation. Facts reported by witnesses, unless substantiated by personal examination, may have no substance. Hasty and impulsive conclusions based on inadequate information destroy a manager's effectiveness and undermine his authority.

4. *Pay strict attention to procedure as outlined by company policy or the union contract.* When instructions are given to do something which an employee has the right to decline under the terms of the union agreement or because of his job classification, he may be uncooperative but he is not necessarily insubordinate. If, in the press of an emergency, you cannot adhere strictly to the union agreement and get the job done, explain the circumstances to the employee (and a union representative, if possible) and obtain his help on a voluntary basis. Discipline procedure should be carefully observed before any penalty for insubordination is imposed.

5. *Review the employee's record.* Extenuating circumstances that mitigate an offense should be considered in making a penalty decision. If the employee's prior record is a good one, that too should be given weight in determining his punishment.

6. *Be accurate in the charge.* Insubordination should never be used as a blanket indictment to cover a multitude of offenses, particularly if the employee's misconduct can really be described as one of poor attitude. If an employee is giving trouble but it is hard to describe his offense accurately, the matter should be discussed with superiors or staff experts and their advice followed.

7. *Be calm and objective.* Emotion plays no constructive part in positive discipline. A manager who allows his dislike for an employee to influence him, particularly when making a charge of insubordination, is likely to have his judgment reversed. A decision to impose a penalty should be fair, consistent with both precedent and the union agreement, and in balance with the employee's misdeed.

8. *Avoid entrapment.* A manager should be careful in all his disciplinary acts never to expose himself to the countercharge of provocation. If such a charge can be made to stick, the accusation of insubordination goes out the window.

9. *Admit mistakes.* The manager who owns up to his errors and reverses a decision if it is wrong earns the respect and confidence of subordinates. False pride and fear of losing face have caused the failure of many an otherwise well-qualified manager who simply could not bring himself to admit that a decision he had made was unfair, arbitrary, and inconsistent with employee justice in general.

10. *Identify the reason.* Insubordination is intolerable in any organization. But it must be kept in mind that insubordination is a protest and that, not infrequently, it is a protest against what an employee believes is unfair or discriminatory leadership. The employee may be totally wrong; however, his behavior will be a signal to an alert manager to study his approach to the supervision of people. Perhaps he is not doing his total communication job.

When Management Faces Mass Insubordination

In a democratic society the economic strike and the unfair-labor-practice strike are recognized weapons of organized labor, which has the legal right to use the first in an attempt to enforce its demands and the second to correct a practice it considers inequitable. Such work stoppages, despite the fact that they are in actuality power confrontations between management and labor, cannot be described as insubordination any more than an armed conflict between two nations could be defined in this way.

However, the wildcat, the sitdown, and the slowdown strike do not fall into this category. To start with, officially at least they are unauthorized by the union and generally in violation not only of the labor-management agreement but of the "no strike" provision that it contains. Such work stoppages ignore the formal grievance procedure, and their perpetrators seek to obtain instantly and by force the settlement of issues that rightfully should be decided by the legal methods established by the contract. In addition, both the slowdown and the sitdown have been defined by the courts as illegal strikes. Of course, management has the right to dismiss employees who engage in these activities; but, relying on the immunity of numbers, they do not really expect such reprisal.

There is many a reason for a work stoppage of this kind. It may be a power play within the union; a faction is seeking to assert its authority and place its own leaders in charge of the local, with whose officers it is dissatisfied. Possibly, the belief may prevail that management is using delaying tactics in the settlement of grievances—to the degree that dissident leaders, unhappy about the situation, decide to take matters into their own hands and force a solution through unified and coercive action. Again, the stoppage may be a form of employee protest: A union member, probably a shop steward, has been dismissed; so they walk out, claiming they will not return to work unless he is reinstated. Or the problem may occasionally be deliberate harassing tactics on the part of the union itself, which publicly disavows its members' behavior but claims it is powerless to do anything about it.

If an unauthorized work stoppage is attributable to the last-named cause—that is, harassment—chances are that the union has long-range objectives which will be made known in later bargaining sessions. For the present, the union may seek to wear down management resistance so that it will eventually seek peace at any price. Some managements, in fact, are so weak and vacillating that they acquire a reputation for giving in to union demands; they are the ones that are particularly vulnerable to the work-stoppage strategy.

The railroad industry has had long experience with worker action of this kind. Operating under the Railway Labor Act, with its management decisions in the industrial relations area severely restricted by various governmental boards and agencies which fix prices, wages, and extent of service, companies lack the bargaining leverage that organizations in manufacturing and service industries possess. Therefore, the unauthorized stoppage, whether it takes the form of group sickness, "going by the rule book," or an actual walkout, occurs frequently. Both parties have traditional methods of dealing with the problem; indeed, the procedure has become so formalized and routine that it resembles a classic quadrille. A railroad union or one of its units makes threats, management goes to court and gets an injunction, the injunction is served, and after a day or two of needless expense and lost motion the situation returns to normal. In the meantime, of course, the traveling public takes a beating. But then the public, particularly in metropolitan areas, is so accustomed to bearing up under what Hamlet described as "the slings and arrows of outrageous fortune" that it can take this kind of trouble in its stride.

A company that has bargaining leverage plus well-trained supervisors and executives, and that observes intelligent and consistent industrial relations practices, is not usually plagued by difficulties of this nature. Grievances are promptly and equitably handled, and the union agreement is lived up to in spirit as well as letter. At the same time, such a company is firm and decisive in labor relations matters. It realizes that the union contract imposes responsibilities on both parties and expects the union to live up to its obligations completely. Employees who engage in uncalled-for work stoppages, especially those responsible for fomenting them, do not act under the assurance that they will escape all penalty for their behavior. Nor is the union office a shelter of immunity. The dissident shop steward or committeeman who refuses to abide by the rules of the contract should expect corrective discipline as quickly as would any rank-and-file employee.

This kind of approach to undisciplined acts by groups within the organization is the only sensible course a management can take. Any company that permits a minority of its employees to engage in illegal activities, and perhaps grants them their demands, ' can expect nothing but trouble in the future. Organizational authority and responsibility disappear in the oleaginous softness of appeasement, and employees not only know they carry the big stick but have contempt for a leadership that allows them to get away with it.

The management that wishes to avoid or minimize problems with work stoppage must be decisive and strong. Its policies must be consistent, fair, and well known to all members of the organization, and they must be adhered to as long as they remain compatible with the needs of the time and are in the best interests of each member of the organization. Supervisors and executives, moreover, must enforce these policies uniformly and fairly. This kind of climate fosters the spirit of positive discipline, for it permits the development of individual pride and the pride of contributing to company accomplishment.

Cautions for Front-Line Management

Although what to do in case of mass insubordination is largely a matter which top executives must decide and handle, front-line management has an extremely important role to play here. The supervisor is the company's ears and eyes in such a situation, and he must be trained so that he knows how to fulfill his responsibility. Labor relations authorities offer these recommendations.

1. *Be sensitive to the approach of trouble.* Any manager worth his salt can sense changes in the moods and working patterns of his subordinates. When employees are unhappy, discontented, or frustrated, their feeling is usually reflected in their attitudes and complaints. If there is a sudden rash of grievances, if people are sullen or surly, if the shop steward is unusually truculent, the wise manager tries to find out why. His advance warning of a coming storm may give management time to head off a wildcat walkout. At least, the company will know what to expect and can be prepared.

2. *Understand the internal politics of the local.* The power of union office has great appeal to certain employees. A natural leader or a would-be leader may chafe under the management of a union officer who he does not consider is as aggressive or militant as he would like. If he is able to persuade other employees to adopt his point of view, he may attempt by the ballot-box method to gain office. Or he may use more direct means to secure power: finding an issue, perhaps, on which he can capitalize, winning employee support for the cause, and then leading his followers to the streets to win his objectives and in this way prove his fitness as a leader. Management should certainly be aware that this kind of person is a possible source of trouble, including illegal strikes.

3. *Analyze grievances.* So long as grievances are normal and relate to the typical differences between management and employees, a supervisor can usually settle them. But when there is a sudden flood of grievances, all connected with a particular issue that has hitherto not been too much

of a problem, the union may be exposing its long-range objectives. Perhaps it plans to incorporate a demand for a specific change in working practices in upcoming bargaining sessions. True, an individual manager cannot do much to adjust grievances of this kind, but he should be able to identify them and report them to his superiors. It is important to do so. Unions have been known to manufacture issues to stir up wildcat strikes and slowdowns so as to give emphasis to certain bargaining demands and, by the very occurrence of such work stoppages, to demonstrate employee support for what the union is asking.

4. *Warn employees of the consequences of illegal strikes*. No employee should be allowed to take part in an illegal strike without a full understanding of the risk he is taking. This includes both rank-and-file union members and officers. Everybody should be made to understand that he is acting in violation of the contract, that he may be exposing his union to a damage suit and himself to dismissal, and that any complaint he has, or thinks he has, can be taken to the grievance procedure for proper adjustment.

5. *Identify ringleaders*. It is quite true that it may be difficult to terminate every employee in a department because he has participated in a wildcat strike. But the fomenters of such a strike can be so punished if they can be identified—and front-line managers are in the best position to name them. More and more, companies are coming to believe that, if possible, strike leaders should be warned before they act that they are known and will be punished. At arbitration, leaders of illegal strikes will undoubtedly claim that the penalty of dismissal is discriminatory because other people who did the same thing escaped with lesser punishments. However, arbitrator after arbitrator has ruled that management has the right to punish the

leaders of a wildcat strike if it can be clearly established
that they were, indeed, the ringleaders.

6. *Penalize the persons responsible.* The management
that decides to take action against the leaders of an illegal
stoppage should inform the union that it expects it to live
up fully to the agreement and exercise its every influence
to bring the work stoppage to a halt. It should underscore
its belief that those who are responsible for the illegal
stoppage should not be excused, regardless of position in
the union; that it does not intend to try to placate people
who resort to force when legal and established means of
securing justice are available. The decision to impose
punishment, in the last analysis, will be up to overall management; but, once that decision is made, individual
supervisors and executives should play their part by giving
the company the information it needs to make any penalties it inflicts stand up as fair under any objective
scrutiny.

7. *Get things back to normal as quickly as possible.*
When the trouble is over, no matter how those involved
have been dealt with, a manager should strive his utmost
to restore normality and positive discipline in his group
as quickly as possible. There is no such thing as victory in
a labor dispute, regardless of whether union or company
has successfully achieved its total objectives. The best kind
of settlement any legitimate disagreement can have is one
that satisfies *both* sides. Although the group insubordination that found expression in a particular work stoppage
was not legitimate and had to be handled firmly and decisively, individual managers should remember that all
persons on the payroll are employees of the company in
every sense of the word and should not be subjected to any
form of reprisal. Neither by word nor by attitude should it

be indicated that employees will not be treated fairly in the future because of their past offenses. The manager whose manner and actions reflect a spirit of resentment may build in an employee the belief that his participation in a walkout was justified and so make the restoration of high morale, effective discipline, and group unity almost impossible.

8

THE UNDERSIDE OF THE AFFLUENT SOCIETY

Discipline and the Disadvantaged

Probably no subject, with the possible exception of the high national tax rate, occupies more of the time and attention of government and national leaders than does the perplexing problem of how to eliminate the social ills that afflict the disadvantaged. The question is extremely complex, and tied in with it are such related problems as crime in the streets, worsening race relations, the high cost of welfare, and student unrest. The concern of the public is evident and frequently reflected in the ballot box. This, of course, is of great concern to politicians, who must keep their constituents reasonably happy if they hope to remain in office and whose reaction to public pressure is not always governed by objective statesmanship.

The average middle-class citizen, whose paycheck is deeply slashed by state, municipal, and federal taxes and who constantly reads how his hard-earned money is being spent on expensive government programs to achieve this or that utopian goal is certainly disturbed. His worry and, sometimes, his anger are reflected by the frequency with which he votes down needed school bonds, elects candidates who promise "safe streets" and a tough line against campus radicals, and hopes against hope that somebody somewhere will find a means of reducing soaring welfare costs.

Irrationally, perhaps, he is likely to attribute this latter expense exclusively to minority groups, particularly Negroes, living in city ghettos, whose militant activities have not been neglected by press, radio, or television. This average middle-class citizen dislikes violence, especially if it is directed at him. He probably objects to any government agency's transferring money he has earned to people who, he thinks, refuse to work for it and consider such a benefit—in the words of certain of their most vocal leaders —as "a right, not a privilege." It is at least understandable why he does not always listen sympathetically to leaders who suggest further programs to alleviate the lot of the disadvantaged, particularly when those programs will cost him considerably more money.

Yet a reasonable public attitude is most important if the leadership of this country (political and industrial) is to take constructive steps toward reducing the size of what might be termed the permanently unemployed, and the problem must somehow be put into clear perspective. The entire question is likely to provoke an emotional response from doctrinaire partisans of any political persuasion who advocate special programs and to stir up frustrated rage in many people who simply wish the whole matter would go away and everything would return to peaceful normality. The trouble is that the problem will *not* go away. Although it is of monumental complexity and defies any plan that promises an instant solution, it would be a self-indulgent nation indeed that simply refused to face up to it and work step by step to solve it.

Who Are the Disadvantaged?

When any objective person examines the problem of the disadvantaged, he immediately discovers that there are many misconceptions concerning it. To begin with, the disadvantaged are not exclusively nonwhites living in city slums. Caucasians are in the majority. Such people are to be found in every state and every community of almost any size. The vast bulk of them are far from militant, and many would like to leave the relief rolls for employment but are prevented from doing so by ill health, lack of skills, lack of education, family responsibilities, or old age.

Furthermore, Negroes are doing a great deal on their own to move into the mainstream of society. They are making spectacular advances socially and economically. According to census figures in 1960, only 20,000 Negro families were included in the income bracket of $15,000 or over. The 1970 census will show that 400,000 such families now earn this much, an increase of 2,000 percent. The number of Negro high school graduates has doubled during the past decade, and the number of college graduates has more than doubled.

In other words, an educated Negro middle class is rising rapidly, and its members usually share at least the same economic values as any other group of property owners.

They want to educate their children and provide them with a pleasant home environment. They want protection for their interests, including their ownership interests. And, certainly, they do not look with favor on any hooligans, black or white, who burn buildings, destroy the possessions of others, and senselessly attack the police. The record shows that most Negro families are as peaceful and law-abiding as anybody else, that they are employed at gainful jobs and are paying taxes. It is also worth noting that these same people are quite as anxious as are their white neighbors for safe streets and are voting in ever increasing numbers for officials who they will think will give them such protection. Finally, it is increasingly true that educated people are more willing to accept another person on his merit and not judge him solely on the color of his skin, so that the lines of social prejudice are less rigid than was once the case. This does not mean that all racial prejudice will soon be eliminated, but it does mean that prejudice will cause far less friction in the future and will be a declining factor as a source of unhappy race relations.

Capable Negro professionals have gone far in medicine and law, and in industry the door is opening to the intelligent and talented. Negroes are moving toward top jobs in many major companies, and in some they are already there. Certainly people who have worked so hard and under such adverse circumstances to improve their position in society will not be attracted in large numbers, over the long term, by the activities of hostile militants who represent, at best, a very small proportion of their people and whose methods discredit their achievements.

In other words, it is well to remember for the record, also, that the great majority of eligible American Negroes are gainfully employed and that, by our reasoning, militant leaders ought to be finding their constituency constantly declining. As a national newspaper columnist expressed it, "Statistics show that the old American melting pot, at least economically, is melting away old barriers at a rapid rate. The . . . black militants . . . are arguing a case that has already been won, and not by themselves." To put it another way, the boundaries of the problems that beset the disadvantaged—at least so far as the Negro is concerned— are clearly definable and relate mainly to a comparatively small group. The vast majority are assuring themselves a place in the American economy, and their success they owe not really to the government or to any leader, black or white, but to their own efforts.

The Submerged 10 Percent

Of course, the fact that more than nine-tenths of the Negro population cannot accurately be described as disadvantaged or underprivileged does not diminish the very real troubles that harass the remainder. Black unemployment *is* distressingly high when it is compared to unemployment in other groups. And the difficulty is compounded because large concentrations of blacks inhabit slum areas in cities, frequently attracted there by relatively high and easily obtained welfare benefits. In the slum atmosphere of poverty, crime, and rootlessness, it is no wonder that they frequently are tempted into violent action and are manipulated by leaders, some of whom offer hope of economic advantages that are impossible of fulfillment.

Large cities have historically sheltered more than their share of poor and unfortunate people of all races, creeds, and colors, who sometimes live in conditions that beggar description. Lacking the education and skills needed to qualify for well-paying jobs, and denied schools of a quality that might provide training which would enable them to improve themselves, some of the more aggressive unsurprisingly turn to crime as a way of life while others, apathetic and unmotivated, give way to listless hopelessness.

The poverty problems and relief costs of major cities are not confined exclusively to blacks or other groups of nonwhites. There are plenty of people of all races on welfare, and big-city police dockets include habitual criminals of all ethnic groups. It is hardly reasonable to expect a person coming from this environment to respond to the discipline of society, let alone the highly disciplined requirements of a competitive organization, after a few months of job training and perhaps some preachments to the effect that "this is for your own good." Actually, the fact that some do respond is a more encouraging truth than its negative opposite—that many do not, or even most do not—and should offer some grounds for optimism to all who are really interested in the long-term solution of the social problems of the poor.

No Easy Answers

American industry, which is assuming an ever greater role in the training and employment of the hard-core unemployed, is well aware that the task will be long and difficult and that progress will be slow. Catch phrases and slogans are not enough. The problem almost boils down to one of reaching each individual. For, not only does a chronically unemployed person have to be given the training (and this usually includes basic education) he needs to do a job, but simultaneously he must have instilled in him the pride and self-respect that provide the motivation to make him *want* to do it.

To give each disadvantaged person the personal attention he needs, from the point of view both of understanding him as a human being and of teaching him as a potential employee, is obviously a herculean undertaking. It is even more discouraging when one thinks that for every person who successfully makes the jump from the ghetto to permanent productive employment, eight or nine fail to do so, at least on the first try, and others continue to swell the numbers of the yet-to-be-trained. For all these reasons, it is quite clear that any degree of success will not come unless all groups in society combine in an unrelenting effort to solve the problem. This certainly means help from the leadership of the expanding Negro middle class, who have a vital interest in the outcome of this pressing social issue.

Statistics are easy to quote and often misleading. For example, a statement appeared in a prominent news magazine that the Negro population was growing more rapidly than was the white, and that therefore it was becoming an increasingly valuable asset to the nation. However, an analysis of these statistics reveals that among educated Negroes in upper- and middle-income brackets the birth rate is no higher than it is among whites and may, in fact, be somewhat lower. This would mean that the increase in the Negro population is disproportionately large among the disadvantaged, the uneducated, and the poor, and whether they will be an asset or a liability if they remain disadvantaged, uneducated, and poor is surely open to question.

It is also true that there is a correspondingly high birth rate among white people of minimal or below-minimal earning ability who must rely on government help in order to exist. The same statement applies equally to them. No country in which the impoverished, under-privileged, uneducated, and irresponsible are becoming a larger and larger part of society can be said to be on the highroad to splendid future achievement.

What Industry Is Doing

Activities of this kind have occurred in Philadelphia. A company executive of this city has been quoted as saying, "Great good is accomplished when an aircraft company builds a plant in Watts and provides employment and opportunity for the residents of that community. We have done similar things here in Philadelphia, and we are quite proud of some of our accomplishments. But we can't be overly optimistic, for we have merely scratched the surface. Black capitalism is all right for the man who has the training and desire to run a business. But it's not much help to a poor fellow who can't read and write and would be unable to make change properly if he were a clerk at a newsstand."

The key to the problem, thinks this executive, lies in the answer to the question, "How do you build self-pride, self-respect, and high incentive into a person who not only lacks these qualities, but may have no real understanding of what they mean?" No one now in government, industry, or education has provided anything but the most tentative answers to the question, and many of the programs that have been developed to translate these tentative answers into action have been obviously wrong. However, the fact that progress to date has been very limited is no excuse to stop trying.

Planning Is Essential

The task of introducing untrained, poorly educated, unmotivated men and women into the highly disciplined, unfamiliar, and sometimes hostile environment of a business organization is a difficult one and requires careful planning. If it is done too hurriedly, an employer is likely to have an experience like that of a Midwestern insurance company whose president gave orders to hire a specific number of people and put them to work. The selection methods were sketchy and preparation for receiving the newcomers almost nonexistent. So, on the day when 21 underprivileged persons began work, the trouble started. There was resentment on the part of many of the firm's regular workers, and some supervisors and executives viewed the experiment with alarm. The new employees themselves were far from happy. After the first day two quit. During what was to be the orientation period there were arguments and fights between regular employees and the new people. One woman member of the latter group in a fit of temper tried to use a knife on a companion. There was an incident involving an employee's reporting to work under the influence of narcotics. All of this was accompanied by a rash of petty thievery; and, worst of all, at the end of six weeks only three of the original 21 workers remained on their jobs. Within another month, one of these had quit.

Everything considered, the program was a disaster, but in the cold light of reason it had no chance of being anything else. Without careful planning, sensible selection, patient training, and sympathetic supervision, a program of this kind has little likelihood of accomplishing any significant results. Even if a plan of action is worked out with meticulous attention to detail and includes all necessary ingredients, there will be many disappointments in trying to carry it out.

A vice-president of personnel for one of the major New York banks, whose institution has won wide recognition for the conscientious effort it is making to bring high school dropouts and ghetto residents into productive employment, cautions, "Don't expect too much too soon! If you hire people who have grown up in slums it is not surprising that their attitudes and behavior don't change overnight simply because you have given them training. It's discouraging when you think an employee is making progress to find that he has robbed someone's locker, been insubordinate to a supervisor, or simply failed to come to work for three or four days. But you measure the success of such a program, not by the number of its inevitable failures, but by the count of people who finally 'make it.' As time passes, this number increases and their influence and example help many of the others who are still trying."

The Humane Approach and a New Opportunity

What to do about the slum dweller and the hard-core unemployed is not a new question. The only new thing about it is that today mankind, at least in Western nations, is trying to answer it in a humane manner.

In seventeenth- and eighteenth-century England, such people were dealt with quickly and abruptly. Gibbets had plenty of customers—men who reached what might be described as the end of their ropes for petty crimes, many of which today would call for no more than a reprimand. The Duke of Wellington's army, which finally brought Napoleon's empire crashing to the ground, included jailbirds, vagrants, debtors, and other unfortunates who could hardly be described as volunteers for "king and country." It is said that when Wellington first saw a draft of some of these recruits he was asked by an officer, "Do you think old Boney will be afraid of these fellows?" "I don't know," replied Wellington honestly, "but *I* am." The American colonies received a goodly supply of their inhabitants from the jails and city streets of England. The mother country was glad to get rid of such undesirables.

But, in the case both of Wellington's army and some of the American colonists, harsh discipline brought order. The early settler, for instance, was in a sink-or-swim situation: He had to work or he did not live. Leadership was stern, and there was little help except what people could provide through their own resources. Not surprisingly, many of these people did extremely well. Why? They had something unbeatable going for them—an opportunity to get a new start in a new country where a person's past position or social standing did not automatically deny him success.

In the social environment of contemporary society, the idea of applying repressive discipline to reduce the problem of the disadvantaged is rightfully repellent. But the positive factor of "new opportunity," taken advantage of by many of the early settlers, is still the only real answer to this perplexing question. Once a person sincerely believes that he has a chance to help himself, he acquires the incentive to learn the skills or take the training necessary to do so, and this is the first step toward self-discipline. However, the goal toward which he is working must be one he really wants; otherwise, the effort may not seem worth the trouble.

The Other Disadvantaged

The mountaineer living in pastoral seclusion on the slope of "Old Baldy" is just as disadvantaged in terms of economics, education, and medical services as is the dweller in the city ghetto. He probably is not too law-abiding, either, if he is judged by the sophisticated standards of the city. On the other hand, he is not a member of a pressure group, he makes no demands, he does not take part in riots or mass demonstrations, and if he manufactures his own illegal whiskey it is of small concern to the public at large. Therefore, despite the attention that is called to his difficulties by congressional representatives of states where he may live, very little is done to help him on a sustained basis.

There are still other categories of disadvantaged people whose troubles pass largely unnoticed because they are not vocal. Taken together, they constitute a problem of enormous dimensions. To persuade such people to accept the same values and standards as the majority of Americans, it would first be necessary to educate many of them to appreciate those values and standards. However, if they live in remote areas, it is doubtful that they will get much attention in the immediate future. The public's attention is focused on the danger spots; that is, those areas where large numbers of underprivileged people live in close proximity to their more fortunate neighbors and resent the affluence which they do not share.

Understanding the Underprivileged

It is impossible to assist the underprivileged and get them off welfare simply by offering to help. Eugene S. Callender, former deputy administrator of New York City's Housing and Development Administration, observes: "An offer to help, even with the best intentions in the world, may only provide this kind of person with one more chance to fail." Companies which are making progress—somewhat slow, to be sure, but steady—in training disadvantaged persons have had the common sense to base their programs on an understanding of the people themselves and of the environment in which they live.

Guy B. Ford, vice-president of the Gillette Razor Company, recently told an audience of businessmen, "Success in hiring the hard-core unemployed depends on the skill of the transition instruction they receive plus the understanding and cooperation of supervisors.

"It is patently obvious that it would be impossible to recruit a person who could be described as chronically unemployed and to put him on a job and expect him to do it. There has to be intense and thorough preparation; in fact, the employee probably has to be taught how to do basic arithmetic and how to read simple English. Furthermore, supervisors have to be trained to direct such people by executives experienced in training programs of this kind."

Any manager who is asked to train disadvantaged people must have a sympathetic understanding of the following facts.

1. A person who lives in a slum and has grown up in conditions of poverty, with violence and crime close at hand, does not think like the average employee. Acts of behavior which repel a middle-class citizen are not so abhorrent to him; he may think they are not even unusual. If he lacks ambition and appears entirely unmotivated, it may be because he does not think he has a chance to succeed. He may not even have the ability to express himself clearly. Security or pride of ownership is foreign to him.

2. This kind of person has no consistent job record. His references cannot be checked by calls to previous employers. He may be familiar with the insides of jails, he undoubtedly dislikes the police, and he may have committed serious crimes or have been suspected of them. The only work he is immediately qualified to do is menial, and this he may resentfully reject on the basis that it is foolish to work for, say, $70 a week as a dishwasher when he can make twice that much selling numbers, pushing narcotics, or just plain stealing. He has no fear of social stigma if he is caught and imprisoned. In his society a sentence in the penitentiary may be a badge of honor.

3. The slum resident may have no understanding of time or regularity. The night may be his day, and the need to get to a regular job at an exact time may be a strange conception. Because he cannot even visualize, much less understand, a permanent productive career leading to advancement and greater economic advantages, the desire to

answer the alarm clock's call early in the morning may be totally lacking.

4. The chronically unemployed person may be hostile to society. It is his natural enemy, especially the middle-class people of any race, even his own. He may think it has cheated him out of the education and affluence which it possesses. Certainly many of his leaders tell him so, and in harsh, unpleasant words. He lacks confidence in his ability to compete because he is painfully aware of his limitations, although he may try to conceal his lack of confidence by belligerence of attitude and antisocial behavior. He may even take a savage satisfaction in frightening what his leaders describe as the "white power structure" by joining his fellows in violent mass action.

Obviously, this description is not applicable to every person who is disadvantaged or who lives in a slum. Many are sincerely anxious to improve their lot; they ask only for the opportunity of self-improvement through productive employment. Nevertheless, in varying degrees these attitudes do affect slum dwellers and influence their behavior.

Experts who have worked in the field have provided this realistic appraisal of city-ghetto residents, adding that any company that embarks on a program to employ them should have a clear understanding of what it is up against. While not all, and perhaps only a few, of the employees recruited will possess the extreme views of the activists or be totally irresponsible in their behavior, some of them will. But any manager who makes judgments based on the actions of some disadvantaged persons and on the strength of this condemns the others has no chance of rehabilitating anybody. The disadvantaged person, like anybody else, has the right to be judged individually. When he commits offenses against discipline, the extenuating circumstances of his background should be taken into consideration so long as he shows by his progress that there is a reasonable chance of his eventual success.

The challenge to industry—indeed, to all conscientious citizens—is to reduce the problem of hand-out welfarism which has alienated large groups of people from productive society. It is a challenge that the country in its own self-interest must meet. Again, the task of instilling the motivation of positive discipline in the new recruits falls heavily on line management, particularly those supervisors who will direct them on a day-to-day basis. Therefore, the end results of any program for employing the disadvantaged will depend on the skill, patience, teaching ability, and perceptive understanding of front-line managers, and all who are asked to undertake such an effort must be carefully trained themselves for the assignment.

From Disadvantaged to Productive Employees

Companies that have had experience in bringing disadvantaged people into their organizations and making them productive employees have learned much about what a manager should and should not do in training such employees. The following suggestions are a summary of their instructions to supervisors.

1. *Remember that patience is a necessity.* The chronically unemployed person is usually deficient in even rudimentary education. He may have trouble understanding the simplest of orders. His vocabulary is different, and words in the everyday conversation of the average employee may be strange and incomprehensible to him. To

compound the problem, his attitude may be defensively hostile, possibly because he expects hostility and rejection. The trainer's first job is to build the worker's confidence through communication and encouragement. This means he must use language that is mutually understandable.

2. *Make the worker a part of the organization.* In the unfamiliar environment of a productive working unit, this kind of employee instinctively feels himself an outsider. He is being asked to cope with situations which he has never before faced and to deal with people who have different values and standards. Simultaneously he is required to discipline his mind in order to master needed skills or acquire specific knowledge, and because they have never been used this way his mental processes may be sluggish and inefficient. However, if such an employee can be teamed with a sympathetic veteran who is willing to help train him and knows how to do it, his progress will be faster. Industry has discovered that this "buddy" system often gets good results.

Whether or not other employees should be told in advance of the arrival of a disadvantaged person in their midst, and in this way prepared for it, depends on specific situations. Some companies keep such an employee apart during his special transitional training, and he does not join the regular workforce until he has completed that training. Then, when his training is finished, the new man is treated like everybody else. If, however, the introductory training is to take place within the framework of the organization, the rest of the employees should be told what to expect and their support requested. Otherwise there may be unnecessary and preventable hostility and resentment on the part of veterans, and it will be difficult for a hard-core person to succeed if he thinks that all his associates are hoping he will fail.

3. *Avoid the do-good approach.* If there is one person the chronically unemployed person knows about and resents it is the "do-gooder." He has been patronized by experts. Social workers have probed into his private life, and moralists have tried to improve him. No one is happy if he is on the receiving end of a charity handout. The disadvantaged person is hardened against moral preachments, and exhortations roll off him the way rain rolls off a slanted roof. But in many cases he can be trained to be a productive employee, and any person whom a company can pluck off a relief roll and add to a permanent payroll is an encouragement to others. Besides, a program of this type is not simply for the good of the poor; it is for the good of society. It makes the streets just that much safer and relief costs just that much lower.

4. *Do not expect the ghetto resident to have middle-class values.* Such a person may be irresponsible and undisciplined if measured by traditional standards. Since he does not know what it means to live within a regular income, when he gets his first paycheck he may spend it foolishly. He may quickly get into debt by overextending his credit. But then, because he has never before had a regular payday, he just does not know how to budget. It is no wonder that he buys things he cannot afford and invests in luxuries instead of necessities. At first he may be a headache to management because he is in constant credit trouble and the personnel department must cope with numerous wage attachments. All in all, the training he receives must be more than job training or skill training. He must be taught how to live, and this must be done tactfully by example and advice, seldom by lecture.

5. *Look for particular skills or abilities.* Job placement is especially important in training disadvantaged people. Many have skills or talent—sometimes latent—that can be valuable if identified and developed. To uncover any such potential takes perception on the part of a manager. Above all, it is essential to place this kind of worker on a job he has the intelligence and ability to be trained to do. If he gets in over his head, he is likely to quit because he lacks the self-discipline to keep trying in the face of discouragement. He may not have the verbal ability to explain his problem to his boss and ask for a transfer; in fact, he may not even think a transfer is possible.

6. *Provide close supervision.* The underprivileged worker needs close individual attention and constant on-the-job coaching. He learns by doing, not be reading or listening to instructions. Initial progress may be discouragingly slow and frustrating to both the employee and his boss. And there will, unfortunately, be failures. But many major companies have already transformed hitherto unemployable people into useful employees.

The key to success in this effort is to understand both the general and personal problems that bother these people. This means studying each disadvantaged person who is being trained and working with him as an individual and a human being.

9

THE REMAKING
OF HUMPTY-DUMPTY

Positive Discipline Reinstituted

W<small>HEN A SHIP IS ON COURSE</small>, a light hand on the wheel is all that is necessary to keep it there. The same can be said of a company or a department that operates in a climate of positive discipline. Its leadership is firm, fair, and competent. Employees accept and respect the authority of their superiors because they have confidence in their leaders' judgment and in themselves. Objectives are clearly defined, policies precisely stated and understood, and communication effective. Each member of the unit has pride in its accomplishments and in his personal contribution to its success; therefore, cooperation comes naturally.

But, when positive discipline breaks down, to restore it is the most difficult task with which a manager is ever confronted. By losing the confidence of his subordinates, he loses their support. In such a situation dissension, insecurity, and loss of direction automatically prepare the way for the rotting away of positive discipline in the group. The circumstances are ripe for a take-over by all kinds of self-appointed leaders; and, although such leaders personally may not command much support, they usually can rely on a highly motivated, intense, hand-picked band of followers who will carry out their orders with force if necessary. So it is not surprising that these leaders can impose their will on a passive majority which has no clear goals and nobody else to turn to.

When this happens in a country, it constitutes a political upset—in extreme cases, a revolution. When it happens in a company, it may mean the assumption of authority by a new management group, by stockholders who have won a proxy fight—or by a militant union. In any event, it is likely to be preceded by a failure of positive discipline.

When Discipline Breaks Down

A loss of discipline may indicate a decline in the confidence of employees in the attainment of the goals that their leaders have set for them or even their objection to those goals. As a result, they no longer respond enthusiastically to their leadership, which they think no longer serves their interests.

Such a loss may also be the result of years of success which have bred organizational softness and complacency. When the unexpected crunch of competition comes, management reacts with confusion and indecision. The employees it has failed then become bitter and resentful and, in their frustration, lose all sense of personal responsibility.

Outside factors—for example, the introduction of a militant labor union into the organization—likewise may lead to the disintegration of positive discipline. Of course, it can also be said that such a union, or even a dissident management group, would have little chance of success in a firm whose employees were satisfied and positively motivated; and this is largely true. Any ambitious group must first find sources of discontent which it can turn into issues that will attract supporters before it can make progress.

However, there are always sources of dissatisfaction, even if they are trivial, in any sizable organization. Moreover, these can generally be magnified and converted into causes which will win sympathy. They can even represent underlying issues which would probably not arouse the least bit of sympathy (if, indeed, people were aware of them). That is why leaders—and often leaders who keep their real objectives hidden—can achieve such astounding results in terms of mass reaction. And it is why the successful company management responds quickly and intelligently to complaints and grievances and endeavors to adjust them satisfactorily while they are only small problems. This kind of management knows full well that to brush aside these minor expressions of employee unhappiness as having no consequence, and therefore not worth bothering about, leads straight to disaster.

Critics—some of whom are esteemed members of the academic profession itself (for example, a former chancellor of Columbia University)—have observed that a major cause of the recent breakdown of discipline on so many college campuses was complacent and inaccessible college authorities. Administrations were indifferent to the demands of students for changes that would make their courses more relevant to their needs; unresponsive faculties concentrated on graduate studies and their own research and consulting activities, leaving such banal tasks as the teaching of undergraduates to overworked graduate assistants.

The humiliation of the American college—its buildings seized by militants, deans and presidents imprisoned in their own offices, classes disrupted, unpopular speakers hooted down and sometimes physically abused, commencement exercises derided and broken up—is a widespread contemporary reality. Whatever may be the reasons for it, certainly it typifies the breakdown of positive discipline in many institutions. The very mortality rate of college presidents is clearly a vote of no confidence in their ability to restore order.

And that, so far as any leadership is concerned, is the real tragedy of the dissolution of discipline within an organization for which it is responsible. If discipline slides down too far, in all likelihood the leadership will be replaced and never have the opportunity to try to return things to normal. A baseball or football team replaces its manager or coach, a nation its government, an army its generals, and a company its top management, with the newcomers frequently making wholesale revisions in the subordinate managerial ranks of the enterprise, probably on a not too selective basis.

Such a reaction is understandable. The old leadership has demonstrated its incapability; hence new leaders must be called upon who will try new methods, new approaches to putting things right—and, it is hoped, exercise their authority in a firmer and more confident manner. Sometimes these new leaders overreact and compound the problem until it becomes almost insoluble. But any leader who is faced with the disintegration of discipline knows immediately that he will never resolve his dilemma with halfway measures, appeasement, or wishful thinking.

Signs of Disintegration

These are some of the conditions a manager may face when discipline has distintegrated:

1. Employees have no confidence in management; some are even actively hostile.
2. Production is down; employees are indifferent to their work, and morale is low.
3. Communication is no longer effective.
4. Supervisors and higher line managers are unsure of their authority and afraid to exercise normal disciplinary measures when employees fail to perform satisfactorily or do not observe plant rules and policies. The reason is that they are uncertain of the support they will receive from superiors.
5. Top management has lost its will to manage, an attitude that is reflected throughout the entire managerial organization.
6. Union officers (if there is a union in the plant) assume authority that they do not possess under the terms of the agreement. Since they may be allowed to do just about as they please, they can hardly be blamed if they become more arrogant and unreasonable in their demands every day.

7. There are frequent acts of insubordination. Failure to carry out orders, idleness, visiting, and other indications of unrest and lack of discipline are rampant.
8. The management team itself has lost all sense of cohesion and teamwork. Cliques form; arguments between associates are frequent and bitter.
9. Capable executives and supervisors (those who have not already left) are casting around for other jobs. The same thing is true of many good employees.
10. There is a general atmosphere of sullenness and resentful despair throughout the organization.

What to Do

Always, such a situation must be handled with a mixture of intelligence, sternness, justice, and skill in communication that attracts support from a large group within the organization and isolates the remainder who are beyond hope of saving.

"To restore discipline to an organization that has lost its cohesion and sense of direction," said an executive who has earned his reputation by putting sick companies back on the road to health, "your first job is to give encouragement to those persons in the company who may hope that finally something worthwhile may be done. Next you must carefully identify those people who, under the right kind of leadership, can make a contribution toward getting the job started. The others, who have quit trying or who have simply become trouble makers, must be dismissed. This can't be done overnight because, in the interest of justice, everybody is entitled to a fair shake. At the same time, you can't be so afraid you'll make mistakes that you're overcautious and delay making decisions that need to be made with reasonable promptness."

Vince Lombardi earned a reputation as a magician of the gridiron when he transformed the Green Bay Packers from long-time losers into perennial professional football champions, but even his most enthusiastic admirers made no claim that he was easy to work for. Moreover, the collection of athletes that he had inherited had lost their morale and spirit, and this was reflected in their relationship with their former coach and in their indifferent style of play.

When Lombardi took charge, he quickly let everybody know that he had come to win and that their job was to play football. It was made clear that there would be no room for players who, no matter how great their potential talent, would not give their best. Lombardi's training program, stressing fundamentals, was long and hard, and he was a relentless taskmaster. But by the force of his leadership he instilled in his players the belief that they could win, and the team began to do just that. The players may have dreaded the hard, long practice sessions, but the results were worth the effort in terms of victories and larger bank accounts.

Lombardi was ruthlessly fair. The story is told of a star Negro player who was asked if Lombardi discriminated. "Mr. Lombardi," he replied, emphasizing the "mister," "does not discriminate against anybody. He treats us all like dogs." This was humorously intended, for Vince Lombardi had earned the respect and confidence of his players. They understood why his standards were high, and they accepted his philosophy that "winning is the object of the game" and made it their own. Those that did not went elsewhere. Furthermore, Vince Lombardi convincingly demonstrated to his team that economic benefits come from being champions. That, together with pride in being a part of a stand-out group, provided all the motivation that was needed for them to win four straight league championships.

An old-line manufacturing company that had been racked by labor trouble for many years was finally forced into such a desperate profit situation that the board of directors, goaded by two or three prominent stockholders, replaced its entire top management. With the help of consultants a new executive team was called in to do what it could to pull the company out of the hole. The new management almost immediately decided that the situation, as it existed, was almost beyond repair. Productivity had declined to a low point, and to all intents and purposes the union ran the shop. The authority of supervisors had vanished; and, worst of all, the company had agreed to extravagantly expensive union contracts which also robbed it of even elementary rights in directing its workforce.

"In this atmosphere," said the president to his board, "we can't hope to accomplish much. Our only chance is to begin to decentralize and start fresh in other areas."

The company spent its last reserves on this venture. At last it began to pay off. Small plants established throughout the nation began to earn money, and more and more operations were transferred to them. Finally, when management had sufficient strength, it was able to face the union over the bargaining table at the home plant and speak frankly. "The agreement has got to be more equitable," it said, spelling out its demands.

A long strike ensued, but management stuck by its

guns. When all was over, even the home plant had been put in a position where it could recapture its prosperity. The entire process took more than 13 years, but in the end management won not only the battle but the confidence of both union and employees.

Said the president when he was finally directing a going concern, "Every step of the way was tricky and dangerous. The attrition in leadership was tremendous. Many employees are gone. I doubt if 25 percent of the people, at all levels, who were on the payroll when we began are here now. For some it was too hard. Some couldn't take the pressure. Some simply did not believe that the old days were over and that we really expected them to give a fair day's work for the good wages they were paid and to meet reasonable performance standards. However, today we have the respect of the union, and our relations with our people are sound. Best of all, we are earning a profit and everybody is more secure. The only sad thing is, none of it had to happen. Any time a management allows conditions over which it has control to deteriorate because it is afraid to exercise its authority cannot blame employees for losing confidence and becoming undisciplined and irresponsible. The leadership did the same thing."

During the early months of World War II, morale in invasion-threatened Great Britain was at a low point and people were in despair. Prime Minister Winston Churchill had little to offer his fellow countrymen except for the famous "blood, sweat, toil, and tears." But his words—plus the promise of action—restored their confidence in themselves.

Franklin D. Roosevelt, telling the people of this distressed nation in the early days of the depression that they had "nothing to fear but fear itself," exuded this same confidence that things would soon be better, that he and the government would make them so. Accordingly, spirits began to revive.

Of course, rhetoric alone will not do the job. It has to be followed up with constructive action. "But," in the words of an executive who took over a near-bankrupt company, "the first thing to do is to give people hope, and words are about the only thing you have got to work with at the start. Then the words have got to be followed quickly with deeds, or you will run out of time."

The Pieces Together Again

To step into such a situation and put the pieces back together again is obviously no job for an amateur. These are the steps that must be taken.

1. *Confidence must be restored.* This can be done only by clearly defining the objectives that the leadership wishes to accomplish and winning employee support for their attainment.

2. *Efficient communication must be reestablished.* Believable communication is based on mutual trust. Employees must be convinced that the leadership is capable and has integrity. They must also be sold on the idea that the goals the company wishes to achieve are possible and that everyone will be given full opportunity to make a contribution to their achievement.

3. *Employees and managers must be judged individually.* Everybody should understand the policies and rules the leadership intends to apply and must realize that each one will be evaluated on the basis of future, not past, attitudes and performance.

4. *The talents, skills, and abilities of all employees, especially those in managerial positions, should be carefully examined.* Many persons whose past records leave much to be desired will respond with outstanding performance under a different type of leadership. In some instances, this may be accomplished by placing them in different or more challenging assignments.

5. *Training must be stressed.* Frequently a major cause of poor discipline is inadequate training. Employees who do not know how to meet performance standards are frustrated and unhappy at their failure, and they may take out their resentment on leaders who did not prepare them properly.

6. *Performance standards must be clearly defined.* Subordinates have a right to know exactly what job standards they are expected to meet and should believe these standards are fair and reasonable. Anyone who thinks he is "working in the dark" and being judged by yardsticks which are unknown or not understood is likely to be unhappy.

7. *The conditions or practices which led to the breakdown in discipline must be changed.* The extreme behavior of certain employees may have been unjustified, but some employee complaints probably had merit. In such cases an intelligent leadership will make immediate changes when possible. If it cannot do so, it will explain why and work toward acting as quickly as is feasible.

8. *Management deadwood must be eliminated.* Supervisors and executives who have lost the will to lead (or perhaps never had it) must be dislodged from the organization for its own good—and even for theirs. Hasty decisions should not be made, and everyone in management should be given ample opportunity to demonstrate his

ability under changed conditions. But persons who obviously do not measure up cannot be permitted to exercise authority if positive discipline is to be restored. In certain instances an executive or supervisor may be near the age of retirement, and his long years of service may entitle him to special consideration. Humane management should be prepared to make exceptions in these and other cases, but in no event should people who have failed in their leadership responsibilities be permitted to continue as leaders. They should be transferred to positions where at least they will do no harm. Early retirement may be a possible solution for some of them.

9. *Continuity is important.* Radical surgery frequently kills the patient. A leadership that takes charge in a crisis situation is usually making a mistake if it attempts instant and sweeping revisions in its management team. It loses touch with the past and deprives itself of the services of many persons who know the problems of the company, understand its operations, and are familiar with the attitudes and abilities of the employees. When a new management assumes power, everyone in the organization, especially supervisors and executives, is bound to feel insecure and uncertain. Intelligent top management will move quickly to reassure subordinate executives and supervisors by explaining its plans, asking for suggestions, and doing everything in its power to rebuild the morale of its leadership group.

10. *Harsh measures should be avoided.* Strong-arm, crack-down methods are not likely to work and may even consolidate resistance. Once sensible and fair rules have been established, they should be enforced uniformly; employees, whatever their past records, are entitled to be judged according to their present behavior. The penalty

an employee receives for violating a company rule or practice should not exceed the gravity of his offense.

11. *Rules should be administered consistently.* It should be made clear right from the beginning that rules will be enforced, policies observed, and all employees treated equally. Firm management does not back away from trouble or attempt to buy peace. It will not appease an unreasonable union or placate a shop steward by letting him play fast and loose with company rules. Probably it will find that it is supported in this attitude by most of the employee group.

12. *Employees must be kept informed of progress.* Everyone in the organization should be given an understanding of the problems that management faces and kept informed of its plans for solving them as these are formulated. Progress should be reported, and the contributions of employees to the accomplishment of management's goals should be recognized and credited.

13. *Front-line management must be strengthened.* The supervisor, once more, is the key to positive discipline. His leadership in large measure determines employee attitudes and motivation, and on his training depends the development of employee skills and talents. He must be a wise policy and rule administrator, an effective communicator and trainer, a knowledgeable labor relations man, and a good counselor. He does not gain these qualities by osmosis but must receive training himself—and it is worth the effort. The way the supervisor does his job will shape each employee's opinion of the company. He deserves the understanding and support of higher management.

14. *"Mood" management should be avoided.* People trust a leadership which is dependable. If a subordinate knows where he stands with his boss, he can do his job with

confidence. An off-again, on-again approach which mixes high-pressure tactics with unexpected periods of relaxation is a good way to destroy positive discipline. Employees do not know what to expect and in their uncertainty become frustrated and resentful. A steady touch and even-handed pressure on the controls are essentials of leadership. A company or a boss who manages by mood will encounter constant difficulty.

10
FUTURE IMPERATIVE

A Look at the Coming Face
of Discipline

WHEN A PERSON attempts to forecast the future, he is too often made myopic by his own experience. The economists of the thirties talked of a "static economy" with a large group of permanently unemployed people for whom the government would have to provide work. Subsequent events proved their pessimistic forecasts very wrong indeed; but, when you consider the climate of the times in which they made their assumptions, those forecasts were certainly reasonable ones.

After heartbreaking attempts in World War I to penetrate heavily fortified German trenches by hurling masses of rifle-carrying infantry against them, the French came to the conclusion that in a future war victory would be determined by the strength of the defense. So they dug a long, deep ditch from Switzerland to Belgium to guard the historic invasion route from Germany, cemented it, enclosed it with a steel roof, and thought they were safe behind their modern Chinese wall, the Maginot Line. The foolishness of the French planning was quickly demonstrated by the sweep of Hitler's panzer divisions around the end of the line, which quickly conquered the country.

In any effort to foretell the future it is logical to analyze current trends, enlarge upon them, and base conclusions on these enlargements. This is, of course, an oversimplification of the process of prediction. Every effort is made by experts to take into consideration countertrends or unknown factors that could throw their predictions off target. But, still, forecasting is a tricky business, for passing years have a habit of knocking predictions into so many cocked hats.

Who Will Provide the Jobs of the Future?

It is obvious that technology is causing tremendous changes in our way of living and in the nature of jobs. In fact, it is reshaping the industrial complex of this country. Since positive discipline is simply another way of describing enlightened self-government in the management of people, it may be wise to examine the predictions many experts are making concerning the extent to which technological progress will affect industry's future manpower requirements.

It is calculated that by 1978 the United States will support a workforce of about 90 to 95 million men and women, or at least 16 million more people than are working today. Unemployment will average about 3 percent.

The nature of the workforce will be greatly changed. Office and other white-collar jobs will exceed those in the shop by better than two to one, and there will be a constantly expanding demand for scientists and engineers. To supplement the work of these professionals, more and more technicians will be required; the increase in these categories of employment may rise more than 50 percent during the next decade.

However, manufacturing companies will not continue to be the great job providers that they have been in the past, despite the fact that productivity will be stepped up tremendously. This last will be accomplished by better machines and better methods, not by more people. In other words, manufacturing firms will offer greater and greater opportunity to white-collar, technical, and scientific personnel, but the number of unskilled jobs will decline. Some experts maintain that, so far as unskilled workers in manufacturing are concerned, employment ten years hence will not rise much above today's level, and in some industries it will actually decrease.

Service industries will step into the breach of declining manufacturing employment and supply more and more career opportunities. The reasons are apparent. Longer vacations, more holidays—most of them arranged in such a way that they provide extra-day weekends—and shorter working days will mean a more leisured population. Travel-related enterprises will flourish and expand, as will employers whose businesses are connected with recreation or the use of free time.

Government, too, will continue to be a major source of jobs. The expanded services of both federal and state governments will provide work for many persons. The U.S. Labor Department says that state and municipal governments will employ about 4 million men and women by 1975, and that is twice as many people as now work for them. The federal government, it thinks, will not expand its personnel so rapidly, only by about 7 percent during the next ten years. But that additional 7 percent will add up to a great number of jobs, for the government of the United States already has millions on its payroll.

The Demands of Tomorrow

If these figures are in any way accurate, they suggest the tremendous challenge that confronts managements in keeping their organizations competitive in the face of change. There must be intensive research on manpower needs, and this includes the training and upgrading of many persons hitherto considered almost untrainable and unemployable. There must be greater selectivity in recruitment, especially for management, technical, and scientific positions. Companies must provide special training for all classifications of employees so they will have the skills necessary to move into more responsible jobs when these are available. Any executive who knows how to adapt the structure of the existing organization of his company so that it will be able to adjust efficiently to coming changes will be urgently needed.

The demands on the executive of the future will be heavy and complex. High wages, high materials costs, high overhead, high taxes, and ever increasing fringe benefits mean that the squeeze on the company dollar will continue, and alert managements will strive to rid themselves of excess personnel weight and deadwood. There will be less opportunity for the mediocre manager to find a safe refuge for himself and, by performing routine assignments, remain in it until he is rewarded by retirement. But—for the executive who has ability—compensation in terms of money, intellectual satisfaction, and a feeling of personal accomplishment will be very great.

According to many authorities, management will "thin out" so far as its top and middle levels are concerned. Machines will replace many human beings who now are assigned to such tasks as routine planning, scheduling, and coordination. This will dig deep into the ranks of middle management, especially in staff departments like industrial relations, accounting, and quality control. But the people who remain in such positions will be able to do their work more effectively and at far less cost.

Forward-looking managements are particularly anxious to attract young people of imagination and intelligence with the competitive instinct to fill their key jobs in the future. For the top executive job of tomorrow will require an unusual man. In the 1950s many companies were willing to allow brilliant scientific theorists to follow academic careers in the belief that average students, if they worked hard, would make good or possibly better executives. This is no longer their point of view, and companies do their best to bring into their organizations bright young Ph.D.'s who have the necessary mental toughness and strength of character to help industry solve the complex problems that confront it. For example, in manufacturing industries high costs are a company's greatest danger, and better technology is the most effective weapon that can be used to reduce them. Therefore, a company needs engineers who can develop better equipment, better methods, and better machines.

The New Executive

Lester R. Bittel, publisher of McGraw-Hill's *Factory Management and Maintenance* magazine, was asked to describe what type of executive would rise to the top of tomorrow's company. He replied, "We doubt it will be the salesman. More likely the top roost will be held in tandem tenure, shared by a finance type looking outward, and a super-engineer looking inward. The money man will be big because of the tremendous investment needed to finance increasingly automatic operations together with the dizzying rate of obsolescence of equipment purchased. His decisions will be the toughest and riskiest to make. He will naturally be in the driver's seat. Sheer complexity and explosiveness of technological means and material of manufacturing presume that a technological expert will share in company leadership."

The company of the future will certainly need the kind of president who can provide practical, realistic solutions to tough, knotty problems. However, he will also have to possess a real talent for building teamwork, loyalty, and cooperation within his organization. In other words, he must combine a deep knowledge of management with an ability to motivate people.

Modern management has long understood that the greater the ability of a leader to encourage the participation of subordinates in at least the implementation of decisions, the greater will be their sense of personal responsibility for the achievement of company objectives. That is why there is such a vigorous effort on the part of alert organizations "to push responsibility downward." Crawford Greenewalt, chairman of Du Pont, commented on the need for the encouragement of individual participation in company and departmental operations when he said, "Give men the maximum of freedom, the maximum of incentive, and the achievements of the individual will be fused into the accomplishments of the organization."

The Problem of Self-Discipline

But, as De Tocqueville long ago observed, "pure democracy does not assure maximum freedom." While an and women who respond positively to the requirements of positive leadership, there must also be a basic philosophy of accomplishment that motivates the leadership of the organization. Otherwise the leadership will lose the respect and confidence of the people it is directing.

Malcolm Denise, vice-president of labor relations for the Ford Motor Company, once said in commenting on the erosion of management's rights, "Unions tend to respect managements which act to preserve their rights." So do employees respect and have confidence in leaders who know what they are doing and exercise their authority intelligently and firmly and consistently. No company can function properly unless employees realize that constructive rules and policies must be voluntarily observed and that, if they are not, corrective action will swiftly follow. In such an atmosphere penalties are a rarity rather than a rule.

Semon E. Knudsen, when vice-president of the Chevrolet Division of General Motors, told a group of students at the University of Michigan, "In business, threat and incentive work hand in hand to keep a man up to his best performance. The threat is veiled in opportunity. Let a man do his job his own way as long as he is successful; if he fails, be tough-minded enough to replace him." Mr. Knudsen added that "the important thing to the organization is that each man be given the opportunity to exploit his talent to the fullest in the way best suited to his personality."

Motivation Is the Essential Ingredient

A certain army general was asked, "How do you motivate men to fight?" He replied, "In every army there is a small group of professionals. They are good soldiers because that's their job, and they take pride in the profession of arms. But most people in any army are not professionals.

"In World War I the Germans marched into France because they disliked the French and wanted to demonstrate their skill as soldiers. They were also motivated by high patriotism. The French struck back savagely because they disliked the Germans and were fighting for their sacred soil.

"Men have fought and died for religious reasons, and today they fight for ideological reasons with the same fierceness. If a person thinks that he cannot live under another man's religious or ideological system, he will fight determinedly.

"Men have fought for survival. The Confederate soldier kept fighting long after real hope was gone because he simply did not want to be beaten.

"But in every case, whether it is patriotism, survival, or fear of the imposition of another man's obnoxious way of life, the leadership of an army has got to understand the

199

sources of its soldiers' motivation in order to capitalize on them."

Managers, like officers in an army, must realize that employee motivation is an individual matter and base their approach accordingly. This will be even more the case in the future as industry relies ever more heavily on well-educated, highly competent specialists to meet its objectives. Such people will expect to exercise greater personal initiative and be managed on a much looser rein than were their predecessors. Extremely competent themselves, at least technically, they will demand competence in their superiors and are likely to be harsh critics of those superiors' faults.

Changing Organizational Structures

Many management experts predict that the organizational structure within which management will operate in the future will be vastly changed. Bernard J. Muller-Thym thinks that the multilayered organization will become obsolete with computerization so that "one can go directly, or almost directly, from any action-taking, decision-making, information-handling points to other points."

And Jay W. Forester, writing in the *Industrial Management Review,* even predicts the elimination of the superior-subordinate relationship. He says that individual profit centers (with individuals or small work teams set up as decision points responsible for the activities in which these centers are concerned) will evolve. "With such a restructured system," Forester believes, "information will be directly accessible to persons who must now operate with too little information either to permit good management or to establish a feeling of security and confidence."

In making his forecasts, Mr. Forester confesses that these changes may be what he hopes to see instead of what will actually take place, but he points out that "data processing, instead of being incompatible with greater freedom of the individual, actually makes it possible because the data base can define the rules of the game, permitting each organizational member to know exactly where he stands and where he can go."

It does not seem likely that the subordinate-superior relationship will really disappear; after all, an organization comprised exclusively of cooperating managers, with no one calling the signals, is difficult to imagine. Undoubtedly, technology will reshape organizational patterns, and changing times will make changing demands on the technical competence of leadership. Fundamentally, however, the superior-subordinate relationship will surely remain the same. It will always be the manager's job to plan, direct, organize, control, and decide—regardless of how much help he receives from machines. It will always be his responsibility to motivate employees and build into their attitudes the desire for accomplishment. For—money aside— a good employee wants three things: the confidence of his superior, who allows him to do his job in relative freedom; recognition for excellent performance and the chance to advance on merit; and a feeling of personal satisfaction for a job well done.

David C. McClelland has made this point in his book *The Achieving Society* (Free Press, 1967). In it he says, "It is not profit per se that makes a businessman tick but a strong desire for achievement, for doing a good job."

What Industry Offers

The desire for achievement is the driving force that moves men forward to the accomplishment of any worthwhile endeavor. In industry, the rewards for successful achievement go far beyond a large paycheck. Although it is fashionable for many young idealists, and older ones too, to scoff at the profit motive, they are usually anxious to secure, often by government subsidy if possible, the use of the money that profits bring to further plans and projects of their own. Since industry has so much to offer a young man, if it tells its story properly it should have no difficulty filling its recruitment needs from the best of each rising generation despite depressing surveys to the contrary.

In a scientific age, industry offers a continuous challenge to the person who thrives best when dealing with hard mental problems and translating theory into practical action. Industry furnishes the chance to build constructively and to supply mankind with the goods and services it needs. It is the muscle of this country's economy, and the wealth it produces largely pays for government and all its services. And it is becoming an avenue of opportunity for minority groups and the hard-core unemployed, who are taking advantage of its training programs to lift themselves to full participation in every phase of American life.

From this viewpoint, it is difficult to understand why any spokesman for the free enterprise system of America is ever called upon to defend profits. Indeed, strictly in terms of the Marxist goal of "the greatest good for the greatest number," this nation's economy has as yet no serious rivals in the controlled economies of Socialist or Communist states.

Industry Must Lead

This is an age of problems, and swiftly changing social patterns are causing management to move into areas which past generations of businessmen believed were hardly their province. Racial and student disturbances, the internal disintegration of cities, high crime rates, the demands by militants for quick and sometimes fanciful government and industrial action, and what might be described as a widening gap between Negroes and middle-class whites—all are hard realities of life. For its own self-protection, industry must take the role of leader in working out our seemingly insoluble problems. It is moving in that direction, but the road is long and rocky.

Despite optimistic news stories about the building of plants in ghetto communities, the National Industrial Conference Board has released sombre figures on the rate at which cities are losing companies. Between 1958 and 1963 manufacturing jobs in major cities dropped from 31.5 to 27.9 percent; and the rate of decline today, though somewhat lower, is still relatively high. It must be remembered, too, that jobs in manufacturing support such functions as administrative offices, research laboratories, and warehouses—and that these also are headed for suburbia. Obviously this flow hinders progress in the training and employment of the hard-core unemployed who, because of lack of transportation and housing, cannot follow industry to the country.

Industrial Relations News has reported that JOBS is asking the nation's employers to train 238,000 unemployed people within a one-year period. To date it says 1,900 companies have signed contracts to hire and train 69,000 disadvantaged workers, with the Labor Department providing funds to offset remedial education, counseling, and on-the-job training expenses. Of course, many companies have inaugurated training programs on their own initiative, so that there are many more disadvantaged who are being given the jobs and training they need. But, in light of the immensity of the undertaking, the surface as yet has only been scratched. The very slowness of our progress in this direction plays into the hands of those who demand instant action and instant solutions.

Paul Pigors and Charles A. Myers, in their book *Personnel Administration* (Fourth edition, 1961, McGraw-Hill) write, "While social developments were bringing our industrial society to a state of urban crisis, technological advances were changing the world of work. With automation and the systems approach, as with recent social innovations, it is too early to say whether in the long run revolutionary advances will turn out to be advantageous or disadvantageous for the men and women who work in continually changing ways with ever more sophisticated machines and electronic processes. Will top executives take full advantage of the new opportunities for freedom to devote most of their time and energy to innovate long-range planning and to decision making at the level of policy? Will members of middle management, freed from the duties of the 'bucket brigade,' develop their uniquely human capabilities for unstructured decision making and for perceptive personnel administration? Will employees at low organizational levels welcome and make good use of opportunities for job enrichment, and for new relationships with employees at higher organizational levels? Will all employees work together to reduce to a minimum the human difficulties entailed in adjusting to a continuing process of technological change? Will they welcome into the world of work persons whose lack of education (among other handicaps) has caused them to be labeled and treated as unemployable?"

The authors say these questions will be answered by the year 2000, and it can only be hoped they will be answered in a positive and constructive manner. If they are, it will be a tribute to the leadership of this country, and much of that leadership must come from management.

With the many forces at play in America, the decisions that are taken in the next three decades will shape this country's destiny. They will, in fact, determine whether or not Americans continue to enjoy a broad, participative democracy whose self-disciplined citizens, conscious of their responsibility to the public good, can work and prosper in freedom. It should never be forgotten that liberty can be substantially lost, although the symbols of democracy remain to give the illusion of its existence.

The Danger of Pressure Blocs

A nation that is at the mercy of warring pressure groups will eventually seek peace of a sort by committing itself to the rule of strong, authoritarian leadership. So there must always be intelligent compromise in any conflict of interests between groups to protect the rights of the general public if democracy is to be preserved.

Not long ago George Meany, AFL-CIO president, was asked if he did not think organized labor in this country was becoming too rich and too powerful. He replied, "No more than the Catholic Church could become too powerful," and indicated that what was good for labor was good for the country. (A former industrialist who remarked that "what is good for General Motors is good for the country" was immediately taken to task by many citizens who held opposing points of view!)

No group in this country—be it business, labor, or any other—has absolute answers to the many perplexing questions that are now being asked. And every group, no matter how excellent its general aims, has selfish interests which it seeks to protect to the best of its ability. This is only human. But selfish interests must be recognized for what they are and not justified on the grounds of altruism or some other basis arrived at by fallacious reasoning.

Mastering the Discipline Problems of the Future

Fortunately, enlightened executives today are well aware of the responsibility of business to play an increasing part in furthering the social objectives of this country. They also know that their key role as leaders is to motivate employees, just as it always has been and always will be. The demands of jobs may change in the future, and employees may have to be better educated and more highly skilled to do them. This, in turn, may mean that a manager will have to have greater general knowledge and a higher degree of specialized competence in order to succeed. But, still, to activate people the same principles of leadership will always apply regardless of the nature of the policies that reflect them.

1. The organization must have a sound and well-defined philosophy on which to base constructive policies that will describe the objectives of the organization and explain how they are to be attained.

2. It must have self-disciplined personnel who are positively motivated and who respond enthusiastically to the challenge of their assignments.

3. It must maintain standards of performance that are reasonable but high—standards that will be supported by training programs that permit employees to meet them.

4. It must have an efficient organization in which assignments are precisely defined and in which the exact degree of each manager's authority is specified.

5. It must organize an effective system which will assure the quick flow of communications up, down, and sideways.

6. It must develop a sound system of procedures and reports which will give managers "fingertip" control over operations

7. It must have strong, enlightened managerial leaders who, by performance and personal example, inspire in their subordinates the desire to excel.

Specifications for the Executive of the Future

In many respects, the management leader of tomorrow will possess many of the same qualities that characterized the leaders of the past. For the qualities of leadership remain constant, regardless of time or place; only methods vary. However, in the coming decades the positive manager will certainly have to have the following qualifications.

1. *Intellectual curiosity.* Change is coming fast, and new situations and problems are crowding in on old concepts. Tomorrow's executive must be able to meet change

with eagerness and initiative. The leader who is shackled by the past or who is unwilling or unable to abandon past prejudices and worn-out ideas will fail.

2. *A sound education.* This is the age of the college degree, but some degrees are not worth very much. The man who wants to rise in industry should prepare himself with a sound educational background and make certain his degree reflects hard discipline, not easy-to-pass courses leading to high-sounding but meaningless letters after his name. As McGraw-Hill's Lester Bittel observes, "Broader-base education is truly fundamental. Disciplines such as physics and chemistry are receiving emphasis. It is upon these fundamental grounds that important manufacturing careers are being made."

3. *An understanding of the implications of automation to management careers.* Formerly there was a great need for systems experts. The man who was quick with a Gantt chart or expert in line balancing could look forward to a bright career. This is no longer true. Computers and machines can handle systems. The ambitious, intelligent young man should never plan to base his career on work that a machine can do better.

INDEX

ABOUT THE AUTHOR

JAMES MENZIES BLACK has served as Distinguished Lecturer on the faculty of the University of South Carolina's College of Business Administration since 1967. He is a graduate of the University of South Carolina, where he also received his M.A., and he was at one time on the industrial relations staff of Daystrom, Inc. (then called ATF, Inc.) and of Associated Industries of Cleveland. He was Personnel Division manager of the American Management Association, assistant director of personnel administration for the Pennsylvania Railroad, and executive vice-president of the American Association of Industrial Management/National Metal Trades Association before assuming his present post.

Mr. Black is author of *How to Grow in Management; Assignment: Management;* and, for AMA, *Developing Competent Subordinates* and *Executive on the Move.* He is co-author of *Successful Labor Relations for Small Business* and *Front-Line Management,* and he has written many articles on personnel subjects for business magazines and many humorous pieces for such magazines as *The Saturday Evening Post, Esquire,* and the *Ladies' Home Journal.*

Mr. Black is a former member of the Planning Council of the Silver Bay Conference and the Personnel Planning Council of the National Industrial Conference Board. He is a member of the American Management Association.

658.3129
B627

87599

DATE DUE